CONTENTS

Foreword (i)

Excerpts from a speech delivered by Michael Ancram, the Minister with responsibility for education in the Province, to a seminar on environmental education held at Stranmillis College on 12 October 1993 (iii)

Reflections from the Chairperson of the NICC advisory committee for environmental education (iv)

1 Environmental education **1**

Introduction 2
Purpose of the materials 2
The need for environmental education 2
Environmental education defined 3

2 A whole-school approach to environmental education **5**

Introduction 6
Attitudes and values 6
Learning contexts for environmental education 6
The formal curriculum 6
Extra-curricular activities 8
Special events 8
School involvement in community action 8
Whole-school ethos 9

3 Management, policy and co-ordination **11**

Introduction 12
Management 12
Developing an environmental education policy 12
Strategies for a co-ordinated approach 13
Evaluating effectiveness 13

4 Examples of environmental education in schools in Northern Ireland **15**

Introduction 16
Part A: Environmental policy development in schools 16
School A: A small rural primary school 16
School B: A large special school catering for physically disabled pupils
with academic abilities ranging from moderate learning difficulties to above average ability 22
School C: A large co-educational post-primary school 28
Part B: A range of approached to environmental work in schools 37
Introduction 37
Exemplar 1 37
Exemplar 2 37
Exemplar 3 38
Exemplar 4 38
Exemplar 5 40
Examplar 6 41

5 Subject contributions to environmental education 43

Introduction 43
The potential contribution of subjects at Key Stages 1 and 2 to environmental education 44
The potential contribution of subjects at Key Stages 3 and 4 to environmental education 54

6 Sources and resources to support environmental education 69

The Education and Library Boards 70
Governmental departments and statutory agencies contributing to environmental education 72
Non-governmental agencies and voluntary bodies contributing to environmental education 78
Television and radio programmes 90

Appendices 91

Appendix 1: Sample definitions of environmental education 92
Appendix 2: Environmental audit schedule 94
Appendix 3: Membership of the NICC advisory committee for environmental education 96
Appendix 4: Acknowledgements 97

Published by the
Northern Ireland Curriculum Council (NICC)
Stranmillis College, Belfast BT9 5DY
Tel. (0232) 381414 Fax (0232) 666573
ISBN 1 85885 044-4   ©1994

FOREWORD

I n May 1988 the Ministers of Education of the member States of the European Community highlighted the need to .... *lay the foundations for a fully informed and active participation of the individual in the protection of the environment and the prudent and rational use of natural resources.*[1]

The sustainable development of the earth's environments is one of the most important world issues in the 1990's. The publication in 1990 of the Government White Paper on the Environment, *This Common Inheritance*, the United Nations Conference on Environment and Development in Rio de Janeiro in 1992, and many other initiatives from governmental and non-statutory bodies, all emphasise the importance of incorporating an environmental dimension across the curriculum in both primary and post-primary schools. The Minister with responsibility for education in the Province, Michael Ancram, demonstrated his concern for environmental education in a speech delivered at an environmental education seminar held at Stranmillis College in October 1993, excerpts from which are provided overleaf.

Because of the immense importance of the environment to the education and future of our young people, the Northern Ireland Curriculum Council (NICC) commissioned a Research and Development Project from the Western Education and Library Board in December 1989. The Project was intended to investigate:

♦ opportunities for the incorporation of an environmental education dimension in the curriculum;

♦ appropriate approaches, content and methodology to meet the needs of the curriculum and of pupils;

♦ effective work in environmental education undertaken in Northern Ireland and elsewhere;

The project was also required to produce guidance for schools which would include a directory of resources.

This publication is the outcome of that project. It shows examples of much good practice which is already being undertaken in many schools in Northern Ireland. They show how schools can create an atmosphere of respect for the earth and its resources. I hope they will encourage all schools to develop policies and plan a whole-school approach to the study of the environment and help our pupils to leave school as responsible citizens, able to make informed decisions at local, national and global levels.

Catherine Coxhead (Mrs)
Chief Executive

[1] *The Resolution of the Council and the Ministers of Education of the Council of the European Community,* May 1988, European Communities.

(ii)

Excerpts from a speech delivered by Michael Ancram, the Minister with responsibility for education in the Province, to a seminar on environmental education held at Stranmillis College on 12 October 1993.

The first point to stress is that the Department is fully committed to the principle that Environmental Education is a vital part of education and training. Accordingly, provision has been made for its inclusion in the Northern Ireland Curriculum thus ensuring that all pupils will experience it throughout their compulsory school careers. Beyond the statutory curriculum the Department has encouraged schools, colleges and universities to incorporate an environmental dimension as an integral part of the curricular framework.

The aim of any proper process of environmental education should be to give pupils a basic knowledge of what the environmental issues are, leading to an awareness of how those issues can affect their own lives. The education should be broad, covering not only conservation issues, but also development.

This will enable them, in future years, to make informed choices and decisions affecting their lifestyles, and to respond sensibly and responsibly to problems with an environmental dimension. It is unashamedly about forming and changing attitudes.

In the compulsory subject of science and geography, for example the environment is a main component of the programmes of study. Positive values and attitudes towards environmental issues are actively promoted at all levels—local, regional and global—and, most importantly in my view, at the level of the individual and what he or she can do to effect improvement and change.

Environmental education presents a host of issues of vital and common concern, to which people of all ages, races and beliefs can readily relate. As such it offers a wealth of contextual material for teaching every subject. There is virtually no limit to the extent to which its important messages can be reinforced in the classroom.

And nor should the informal curriculum be forgotten. There is a vast range of projects, competitions and other initiatives available to schools covering the whole spectrum of environmental matters. Despite the pressures of change in education at the moment, schools, classes, teachers and pupil groups have continued to pursue such initiatives locally, nationally and internationally. Often these have involved a partnership with statutory or voluntary agencies or the private sector. All initiatives to enhance the environment, to raise awareness or to demonstrate environmental responsibility support what we in the education service are trying to do in schools, whether it be through .... active partnership with schools or simply by good example.

Such headway as we have made in environmental education—and I think it is significant—should not lead to complacency on our part. There is a need for continued contact between voluntary organisations, industry and government departments for the benefit of our young people.

This is truly a challenge which involves everyone. It will be a real test of the commitment and expertise of all .... to find feasible, affordable and engaging ways to achieve further improvement in our provision, and further gains from our investment in environmental education.

Taken from Education in the Environment, *Delivering the Message-Environment Education in Northern Ireland,* Report of a Seminar on Environmental Education, Stranmillis College, 12 October 1993. Belfast: Royal Society for the Protection of Birds.

**Reflections from the Chairperson of
the NICC advisory committee for
environmental education**

*When a blackbird sings outside the window, children
listen and are eager to see him.*

*His notes are truly musical, worth attempting, and
his presence and reasons for singing are worth
understanding.*

*Children are interested in every bird, and flower and
tree that grows in real life, in a nearby corner.*

*They want to see clouds with faces and bodies the
shape of animals; and walk through puddles; and
feel the rain and snow; and listen to every wind that
blows; and pretend an orange is the round flaming
sun.*

As with a drop of stream water and the stream, they find excitement in a single grass and marvel at how many grasses make a meadow.

On hands and knees like rabbits and other animals in long grass, they pick up many scents and feel real textures and see bumbles and wasps and other insects; and don't touch stinging nettles.

They respect the speed of the hare and the daring fox, the shy badger and otter, the flitting bat, the frightened mouse, dangerous rat–in holes in the ground and in walls of stone from hills and cliff faces.

They are interested in fishes and sand and soils and worms, and how people farm the land and the sea.

How people worked and bartered and spoke and prayed and sang and told and wrote stories, and built homes and workplaces and money-houses.

The children grow more interested. So the questions come, until their parents and teachers become as puzzled as the children themselves.

Everybody knows that understanding the nature and value of things, all about, is the essence of true education.

They say, 'Give us something that will begin to make sense of all of these things.'

-Environmental education is that beginning.

OLLY McGILLOWAY

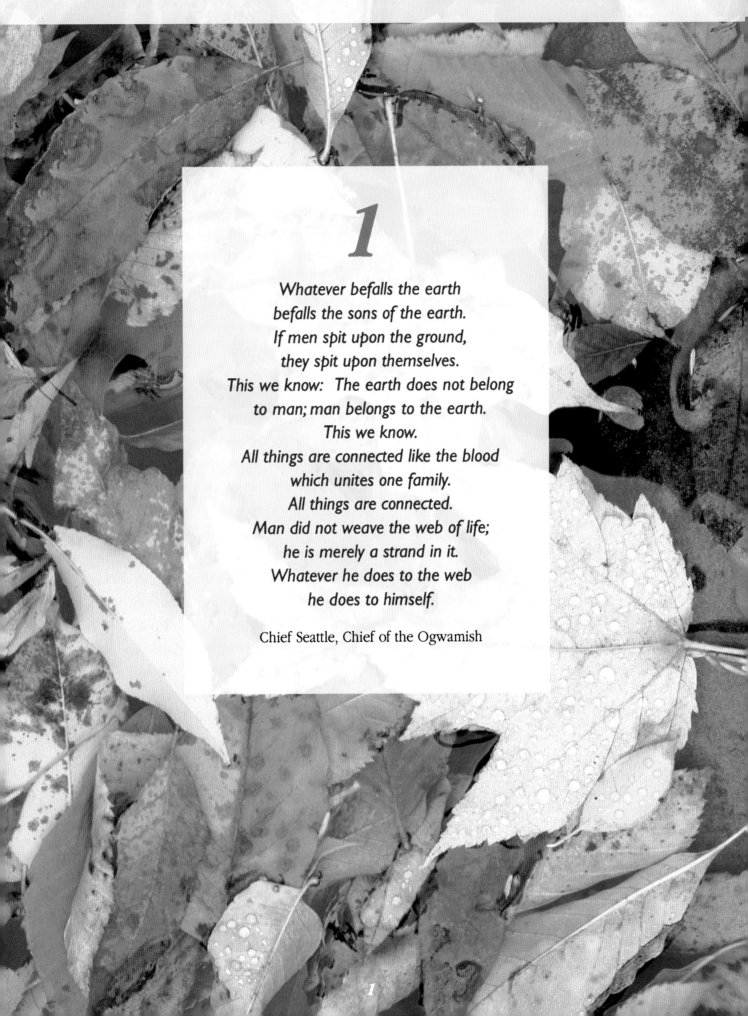

1

Whatever befalls the earth
befalls the sons of the earth.
If men spit upon the ground,
they spit upon themselves.
This we know: The earth does not belong
to man; man belongs to the earth.
This we know.
All things are connected like the blood
which unites one family.
All things are connected.
Man did not weave the web of life;
he is merely a strand in it.
Whatever he does to the web
he does to himself.

Chief Seattle, Chief of the Ogwamish

INTRODUCTION

In 1992 heads of state and delegates from over 150 countries attended the 'Earth Summit' in Rio de Janeiro to discuss world responsibility for, and response to, environment and development issues. Delegates agreed that the only effective way of ensuring the protection and enhancement of the environment in the long term was to bring about change in people's attitudes and behaviour. As a result *Agenda 21*, a 500-page action programme, was drawn up. Of the number of activities agreed the following were particularly pertinent to the education sector.

.... Governments should strive to update or prepare strategies aimed at integrating environment and development as a cross-cutting issue into education at all levels within the next three years.

.... Relevant authorities should ensure that every school is assisted in designing environmental activity work plans, with the participation of students and staff.[1]

PURPOSE OF THE MATERIALS

These materials have been prepared to help schools respond to the need for an increased emphasis upon environmental education. They seek to illustrate how environmental education is accommodated within the current work of schools and within the programmes of study of the Northern Ireland Curriculum.

Section 1 This section sets the scene for environmental education, what it is and why schools should give attention to it.

Section 2 This section suggests that a whole-school approach is essential for effective environmental education. It identifies areas of school life which act as learning contexts for environmental education.

Section 3 This section offers advice on the management of a whole-school approach, the development of policy and strategies for co-ordination.

Section 4 This section provides examples of environmental education undertaken in schools in Northern Ireland. It is in two parts. Part A provides three case studies which illustrate how environmental education is developed as a whole-school approach. Part B provides a range of environmental work/activities undertaken in a number of primary and post-primary schools and illustrates how the activities can be incorporated into curricular work.

Section 5 This section highlights opportunities within the subjects of the Northern Ireland Curriculum which facilitate the development of environmental education as a coherent theme throughout the curriculum.

Section 6 This section provides details of support agencies and further sources and resources which may assist teaching and learning about the environment.

THE NEED FOR ENVIRONMENTAL EDUCATION

The study of the environment has long been part of the educational process in schools. In recent years it has gradually taken on greater significance as awareness of the scale and implications of worldwide environmental issues has increased.

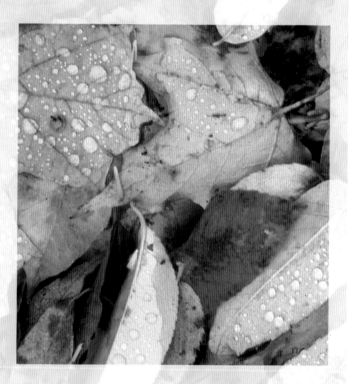

The world has become a global society. Environmental issues cross national boundaries and environmental disasters anywhere can affect a local environment. As a consequence, responsibility is shared, not only for conditions in this part of the world, but also for conditions elsewhere.

Over the last three decades it has become increasingly apparent that the environment cannot withstand the pressures being placed upon it. The quality of life and the survival of future generations will be affected by the attitudes and actions adopted currently towards the environment.

Schools play a vital role in helping pupils to develop knowledge and foster positive attitudes towards stewardship of the environment. The pupils of today are the decision-makers of tomorrow. They need to be equipped with the knowledge and competences to shape and manage the world for which they are responsible.

ENVIRONMENTAL EDUCATION DEFINED

Environmental education can be defined as a process which involves:

♦ developing knowledge and understanding about the environment;

♦ fostering positive attitudes towards management and stewardship of the environment; and

♦ encouraging behaviour and action consistent with sustainable development of the local and global environment.

Environmental education should provide experiences for learning **about** the environment and the emphasis should be, as much as possible, on learning **in**, **through** and **for** the environment.

Learning **about** the environment helps to develop knowledge and understanding on local, national and global scales.

Learning **in** and **through** the environment helps to develop enjoyment of, and empathy with, the environment as well as a range of skills necessary for problem-solving and decision-making.

Learning **for** the environment helps to develop attitudes and values which promote responsible behaviour and action.

Additional definitions of environmental education have been included at Appendix 1. Schools may find these a useful stimulus for discussion.

REFERENCES

1 Taken from Promoting Education, Public Awareness and Training (Chapter 36), *Agenda 21*, United Nations Conference on Environment and Development, 1992. Switzerland: United Nations for the General Assembly.

A WHOLE SCHOOL APPROACH TO ENVIRONMENTAL EDUCATION

2

If you think ONE year ahead – plant rice.
If you think TEN years ahead – plant a tree.
If you think ONE HUNDRED years ahead –
educate the children.

Kuan Izu, Chinese poet

INTRODUCTION

The effectiveness of environmental education is dependent upon the entire school community being aware of, and actively contributing to, the careful use of the environment. Traditionally, much of the focus of environmental education in schools involved developing knowledge about the environment. It is essential that, as well as developing knowledge, the education process also guides the development of attitudes and values which influence behaviour and affect lifestyles.

ATTITUDES AND VALUES

The fostering of positive attitudes and values is at the core of environmental education. The kinds of relationships we develop with the environment will determine the values we hold in relation to it, just as the kinds of values we hold shape our relationships with the environment. Essential features of environmental education include:

♦ an aesthetic appreciation of the natural and built environment;

♦ a sense of belonging to and ownership of the global environment;

♦ an awareness of the interdependence of people and people and nature; and

♦ an awareness of individual social responsibility and the need to respect the collective good.

These features should underpin all teaching and learning in whatever context environmental education takes place. Every part of the school environment and the day-to-day life of the school can be used as a context for teaching and learning about the environment.

LEARNING CONTEXTS FOR ENVIRONMENTAL EDUCATION

The five contexts for learning identified opposite form a framework for developing a whole-school approach to environmental education. Many schools may have developed one or more of these areas already, while some schools may be about to start. Schools will select an area or areas for development, depending upon their particular needs and circumstances.

THE FORMAL CURRICULUM

SUBJECTS AND CROSS-CURRICULAR THEMES

Aspects of environmental education have been written into the programmes of study and attainment targets for many of the contributory subjects of the Northern Ireland Curriculum. The tables in Section 5 highlight the ways in which environmental education has been included, either as part of a specified requirement within the programmes of study, or has potential as a context for study. Teachers may find these tables helpful as a basis for discussion and a stimulus for further development work on the environment.

Some of the objectives of the educational (cross-curricular) themes seek to address issues related to the environment. For example, one of the objectives for health education promotes health in relation to the environment. Education for mutual understanding highlights specifically the need to know about global interdependence and the impact that environmental change can have at a range of scales. The environment is a common heritage and is used by many schools as a context in which to address cultural heritage and education for mutual understanding. One of the objectives for careers education requires pupils to have direct contact with the world-of-work. Through such contacts, pupils may develop an appreciation of how work practices and organisations are influenced by environmental concerns. Economic awareness highlights the need for pupils to appreciate that individuals, as consumers, and those in the business community, have a responsibility to take account of environmental issues in both a local and international context.

TEACHING AND LEARNING APPROACHES

Effective environmental education moves away from teaching and learning approaches based solely on the transmission of knowledge, and moves towards approaches which encourage the development of qualities, such as initiative, reflection and responsibility in relation to the environment and the fostering of attitudes and values which influence behaviour and action. Teaching and learning approaches, such as group work, discussion, debate, role-play and problem-solving can be effective techniques for stimulating and maintaining pupils' interest in the environment.

**THE FORMAL
CURRICULUM**
subjects and
cross-curricular themes
teaching and
learning approaches

**EXTRA-CURRICULAR
ACTIVITIES**
school clubs
membership of national
societies

AREAS OF SCHOOL LIFE
WHICH CONTRIBUTE TO
TEACHING AND LEARNING
ABOUT THE
ENVIRONMENT

**WHOLE SCHOOL
ETHOS**
spirit and atmosphere
parental involvement
physical environment

SPECIAL EVENTS
environment days/weeks
environmental
competitions

**SCHOOL
INVOLVEMENT IN
COMMUNITY ACTION**

local projects
monitoring local issues

The range of approaches and strategies set out below and overleaf offers examples of how teachers might provide opportunities for learning **about, in, through** and **for** the environment.

♦ **Use of real issues**: Pupils respond best to real situations. Issues, such as the impact of a new housing development or the pollution of a local stream can engender interest and encourage pupils to reflect upon real environmental issues.

♦ **Use of secondary sources**: Interest in the problems of unfamiliar environments can be stimulated by the use of videos, photographs, newspaper and magazine articles, and displays in museums and interpretive centres.

♦ **Use of the school grounds**: Pupils need opportunities to realise that responsibility for the earth begins at a local level and that environments can be managed in a manner which promotes sustainability. Introducing pupils to the management of a small area, such as the school grounds, can help to develop understanding of how similar principles can be applied to larger scales and that actions and decisions at a local level can have meaning in a global context.

♦ **Enquiry-based learning**: The environment can be a context for hypothesis-testing or conducting surveys, where pupils can develop skills of recording information, analysis, interpretation and evaluation.

- **Action-based fieldwork**: This involves pupils in practical caring for, or improvement to, the school grounds or the local area. It is a method of raising awareness to the quality of the surrounding environment. It can also provide the challenge of applying principles learned to regional and global contexts.

- **Field trips/fieldwork**: These build on, reinforce and provide first-hand experience of topics or issues explored in the classroom. They involve preparation and follow-up activity, and can include a range of experiences, such as

  - aesthetic and sensory experiences
  - outdoor pursuits
  - enquiry based learning
  - action in the environment.

- **Residential experience**: A residential experience can provide opportunities for a holistic approach to environmental awareness and appreciation. It offers pupils extended opportunities to be part of, and to engage with, the environment over a period of time.

EXTRA-CURRICULAR ACTIVITIES

SCHOOL CLUBS

Pupils can be given opportunities to develop their interest and understanding of the environment outside school hours through clubs which involve environmental activities, such as bird-watching, fishing or rambling.

MEMBERSHIP OF NATIONAL SOCIETIES

Many of the voluntary bodies with interests in the environment organise clubs in Northern Ireland to which schools can be affiliated, for example:

- the Royal Society for the Protection of Birds (RSPB) runs a young ornithologists' club and schools can apply for group membership;

- the Ulster Wildlife Trust (UWT) runs a conservation club known as 'Watch' for eight to fifteen year olds; and

- the National Trust (NT) organises conservation working holidays, known as 'Acorn Camps', all over the United Kingdom for young people over seventeen years of age.

Membership of these organisations can provide pupils with opportunities to experience the natural world at first-hand and also to become involved in worthwhile environmental activities.

Many post-primary schools take part in the Duke of Edinburgh Award Scheme. All pupils who take part in the scheme must undertake at least one expedition into the countryside. Increasingly, opportunities are provided to travel abroad to explore global issues. Schools have found that participation in the scheme helps to foster environmental awareness among pupils.

SPECIAL EVENTS

A number of interpretive and countryside centres run special one-day events, such as 'fungal forays' or 'bat walks'. The Ulster Tree Committee (a sub-committee of the Council for Nature Conservation and the Countryside) is responsible for the organisation of 'Tree Week' involving activities, such as nature trails and tree planting. In support of such activities, or as a school-initiated event in its own right, a school may wish to organise a short, intensive event, such as an environment day or week which will allow a class, year group or possibly the whole school, to devote a block of time to activities with an environmental theme.

ENVIRONMENTAL COMPETITIONS

A number of voluntary conservation bodies and local councils organise competitions sponsored by industry and commerce. These can involve pupils in activities, such as the design of wildlife gardens and nature trails. These can challenge pupils to apply learning derived from a range of contexts to an environmental issue or problem.

SCHOOL INVOLVEMENT IN COMMUNITY ACTION

LOCAL PROJECTS

Schools can avail of opportunities to become involved in local action to improve the environment, such as helping to clean up a derelict site or a local river bank. Interested pupils can volunteer, for example, to carry out a wild bird count, a survey of local pollution or to plant trees to enhance the environment.

MONITORING LOCAL ISSUES

Schools may wish to become involved with monitoring the environmental impact of local developments, such as a new roadway, an extractive industry or a housing scheme. These can provide real life opportunities to evaluate differing viewpoints and conflicting interests.

Schools will recognise that involvement in local issues requires sensitive management. It will be important to:

♦ inform the Board of Governors of the school's wish to become involved;

♦ research carefully and consider all aspects of the issue;

♦ invite interested parties–planners, industrialists, architects or local residents–to put forward their points of view;

♦ assess the implications for the environment and the local community;

♦ suggest possible solutions consistent with sustainable development of the environment;

♦ ensure that action, such as writing to local councillors, Members of Parliament and/or obtaining media attention, is undertaken with the knowledge and support of school management.

WHOLE-SCHOOL ETHOS

SPIRIT AND ATMOSPHERE

The spirit and atmosphere of the school will reflect the extent to which the school is genuinely committed to environmental education and action. Individual and collective responsibility for the school environment can be encouraged through:

♦ making the issue a regular topic at school assemblies;

♦ using school notice boards to display environmental work and materials; and

♦ inviting representatives of environmental organisations to make presentations and stimulate discussions.

For environmental education to be effective, behaviour and action both inside and outside the classroom needs to be consistent with the environmental message and exemplified in the school's approach to issues, such as:

♦ care of the school building and grounds;

♦ energy efficiency;

♦ recycling;

♦ conservation;

♦ purchasing policy;

♦ use of materials and resources; and

♦ disposal of waste.

PARENTAL INVOLVEMENT

Liaison with, and involvement of parents in, the life of the school are important so that environmental messages conveyed in school are reinforced and supported in the home. Parent/Teachers Associations might be encouraged to make environmental issues part of their planned programme of activities which could include, for example, raising funds or giving practical support to improve school grounds.

PHYSICAL ENVIRONMENT

Care and respect for the physical environment of the school is an integral part of school life. It is important that teaching and non-teaching staff, pupils and visitors, all share a commitment to continuous monitoring of the care and appearance of the school environment. This will be reflected in:

♦ a pleasant welcoming reception area;

♦ door mats placed at strategic points;

♦ rooms, corridors and stairs which are clean and in good repair;

♦ adequate heating and ventilation;

♦ clean toilets and changing rooms; and

♦ well-managed school grounds.

Sufficient litter bins need to be available in classrooms, cloakrooms, corridors and playgrounds so that pupils are encouraged to keep these areas litter free. Pupils can be motivated by opportunities to investigate for themselves issues related, for example, to litter control and/or the general improvement of the physical environment of the school.

3

*Greening is about placing a value
on the environment.
It is a holistic exercise which
requires the integration
of an environmental ethic
into both academic
and institutional practice.*

from *Greening the Curriculum,* Committee of
Directors of Polytechnics, 1991, Middlesex

INTRODUCTION

Developing a whole-school approach to environmental education is a long-term process. A school which seeks to promote environmental awareness as a way of life will do so in the context of whole-school planning, management and co-ordination.

MANAGEMENT

For environmental education to permeate the whole curriculum, ethos and management policy of the school, will require the explicit commitment of the Board of Governors, Principal and Senior Management Team. Management may choose to designate day-to-day responsibility to a senior member of staff, a co-ordinator, or a staff working group. Whatever the strategy, the emphasis should focus on environmental education as the shared responsibility of all members of the school community.

DEVELOPING AN ENVIRONMENTAL EDUCATION POLICY

A clear policy statement and code of practice which expresses the school's commitment to environmental education will form a guide for the development of whole-school action. The success of environmental education is dependent upon the support and enthusiasm of pupils, teaching and non-teaching staff, and parents. It is important, therefore, that the school policy is developed through a process of consultation and agreement.

A policy on environmental education might include reference to some of the following:

♦ an indication of the current position;

♦ a rationale explaining why the school considers this aspect of education important;

♦ the contribution of the contributory subjects of the curriculum and from extra-curricular activities;

♦ the contribution of the school ethos;

♦ liaison with outside support agencies;

♦ an action plan;

♦ strategies for co-ordination;

♦ implications for staff and resources; and

♦ plans for continuous monitoring and evaluation.

EVALUATING THE CURRENT POSITION

Figure 1 in Section 2 may provide a useful starting point for carrying out an audit of current provision. The audit will need to take account of:

♦ the contribution of individual subjects and educational (cross-curricular) themes to environmental education. (Schools may find it helpful to refer to Section 5 which offers a summary of the contribution which subjects can make to environmental education.);

♦ the range of learning activities and teaching strategies employed to deliver environmental education, for example, the current provision for fieldwork and visits;

♦ the contribution of extra-curricular activities;

♦ opportunities to promote environmental awareness within school life;

♦ the resources available in terms of library books, video resources, teaching packs;

♦ opportunities for teaching and learning provided by the school grounds;

♦ arrangements for raising staff awareness; and

♦ arrangements for liaison with relevant support agencies.

Consideration also needs to be given to:

♦ the school policy on purchasing, for example, recycled paper, environmentally friendly cleaning materials;

♦ waste management, for example, a recycling programme for paper, cans and bottles;

♦ efficient use of energy, for example, the insulation of windows and doors and the use of light and heat; and

♦ management of school grounds, for example, the effective use of litter bins and the use of organic fertilisers.

Schools may find the environmental audit schedule, at Appendix 2, a useful instrument in carrying out a formal evaluation of their current position.

AN ACTION PLAN

When the initial audit has been completed, schools might consider drawing up an action plan which:

♦ raises whole-staff awareness to the issues;

♦ takes account of existing provision;

♦ identifies how provision might be improved; and

♦ sets out the steps to be taken, the resources needed and approximate time-scales.

STRATEGIES FOR A CO-ORDINATED APPROACH

The Principal may wish to appoint a senior member of staff and/or working group with designated responsibility for ensuring a planned, structured and coherent approach to environmental education. Responsibilities are likely to include:

♦ raising awareness of, and encouraging commitment to, environmental issues among teaching and non-teaching staff;

♦ carrying out an audit of the current position;

♦ drawing up a policy, action plan and code of practice in consultation with the Board of Governors, staff, pupils and parents;

♦ developing an overview of individual subject contributions to environmental education by collating information from teachers/departments;

♦ assisting staff to construct programmes which are complementary but which avoid duplication and take account of progression;

♦ ensuring that all pupils have first-hand experience of practical activities in the local environment;

♦ ensuring that the school's extra-curricular activities include opportunities for environmental involvment;

♦ ensuring that all aspects of school life become increasingly compatible with positive environmental messages;

♦ identifying staff training and resource needs;

♦ keeping abreast of developments in environmental education;

♦ undertaking liaison with external support agencies concerned with environmental education (See Section 6 for sources and resources); and

♦ continuous monitoring and evaluation of the impact and effectiveness of the school policy.

EVALUATING EFFECTIVENESS

Continuous monitoring and evaluation need to be carried out both formally and informally. The effectiveness of a school's policy, action plan and code of practice can be assessed only within the context of each individual school's situation and the targets which the school itself has set. Success will have been achieved if there is increased environmental awareness and action amongst pupils, teaching and non-teaching staff and if pupils have had their understanding, appreciation and experience enhanced by working **in** and **through** the environment.

EXAMPLES OF ENVIRONMENTAL EDUCATION IN SCHOOLS IN NORTHERN IRELAND

4

*Today I would go so far as to say
that the search for economic prosperity,
democracy and peace will fail
unless the importance of conservation
is perceived and taken into account
in all these endeavours.*

Norman Moore, *The Bird of Time: The Science and
Politics of Nature*, 1987, Cambridge University Press

INTRODUCTION

Many schools in Northern Ireland have been involved in environmental education for a number of years. Part A of this section offers examples of how three schools worked towards developing environmental education as part of whole-school policy. While each case study is based on an individual school, some adaptations have been made to reflect the activities of other schools involved in similar explorations. Part B offers a range of activities, projects and initiatives undertaken by a number of primary and post-primary schools throughout the Province. The exemplar work in both parts can be adapted readily for use in primary, post-primary and special schools.

PART A

ENVIRONMENTAL POLICY DEVELOPMENT IN SCHOOLS

SCHOOL A:
A small rural primary school

DESIGNING AND DEVELOPING THE SCHOOL GROUNDS AS A CONTEXT FOR TEACHING AND LEARNING ABOUT THE ENVIRONMENT

Our school is a small rural primary school. Because I have a particular interest in the environment I wanted to develop everyday learning experiences for pupils in the immediate environment of the school and to use it as a learning context for cross-curricular work. The school grounds seemed the ideal learning resource for a starting point.

I discussed the idea with the other teachers in the school and we agreed that:

♦ as many year groups as possible should be involved so that the environment would become part of the daily life of the school;

♦ a long-term development plan should be mapped out, setting targets and taking account of the curricular requirements of a number of subjects;

♦ as far as possible, all pupils should learn **about** the environment **through** direct experience of their own environment;

♦ all pupils should be encouraged to care **for** the environment.

We planned to start by involving the pupils in Years 3, 4 and 5 and decided to set aside one hour on two afternoons each week. As the teacher responsible for Years 3, 4 and 5, I mapped out aspects of subjects I felt could be reinforced and consolidated through practical activities in the school grounds. (See Table 1.)

I decided to draw up a development plan as a basis for discussion with colleagues. The plan outlined a number of developmental stages.

STAGE 1

This would involve:

♦ evaluating the current layout of the school grounds;

- identifiying problem areas;

- assessing the current use made of the school grounds;

- considering the image projected by the school grounds.

STAGE 2

This would involve:

- mapping the school grounds to include play areas, car parking facilities, trees and shrubs;

- identifying features, such as sunny spots, badly drained areas and areas where litter accumulates.

STAGE 3

This would involve:

- informing the Board of Governors, parents and non-teaching staff, and enlisting their support;

- contacting the local Education and Library Board and relevant voluntary agencies for advice and guidance.

STAGE 4

This would involve:

- generating ideas on improvements and developments to the school grounds;

- considering costs;

- devising plans to raise funds.

Working with the pupils we began by looking at the school grounds and listing all our 'likes' and 'dislikes'. Pupils brainstormed ideas for improvement. All of these were discussed and, on the basis of their discussions, we sketched the proposed improvements and developments of the school grounds (See Map 1.) A timetable of suggested dates for carrying out the proposed developments was drawn up. (See Table 2.)

The success of our endeavours was due in no small measure to the support of the local community and the advisory and maintenance staff of the Education and Library Board which provided advice and practical assistance. Conservation Volunteers Northern Ireland (CVNI) also provided advice and practical help with the building of the dry stone wall. The caretaker and the school bus driver helped to build the nesting boxes, bird tables and bench seat. The local brewery provided wooden barrels from which we made our plant tubs, and local farmers supplied manure and stones.

The staggering of events allowed pupils to experience early success which generated enthusiasm and encouraged motivation. It also helped pupils to realise that environmental improvement requires continuous care and attention.

The focus on the school grounds has engendered a sense of community both within the school and in its links with the local area. This has helped pupils to realise that learning **about**, and caring **for**, the environment is not just a school subject but is a matter of concern for everyone and something to which everyone can contribute.

The school grounds proved to be an excellent starting point for environmental education in our school. By working **in** and **for** their immediate environment the pupils have developed knowledge, skills, attitudes and values which, it is hoped, will influence their future lifestyles. In particular, the pupils have:

- developed their skills in collecting, analysing and interpreting information;

- learned to identify factors which affect the environment;

- become more confident in asking questions, defining problems, proposing and evaluating solutions;

- developed their communication skills of observation, description, recording and expression of feelings and opinions;

- learned to discuss issues and make decisions in co-operation with others leading to positive action to improve their environment;

- developed their sense of curiosity, wonder and aesthetic appreciation of the environment;

- become more aware of, and shown greater respect for, the needs of other living things;

- developed their sense of personal responsibility for their local environment.

Future plans for environmental education in our school include carrying out an environmental audit of the school building which will lead to planned action by pupils and staff within the school.

Note: Schools planning to develop their school grounds as a context for learning about the environment may find the following two references particularly useful.

REFERENCES   TABLE 1

Learning Through Landscapes: Using School Grounds as an Educational Resource, K Young, 1990. Winchester: Learning Through Landscapes Trust.

Practical Conservation Pack: Advice for Teachers, Compiled by Conservation Volunteers on behalf of the Ulster Tree Committee, 1987. Belfast: Conservation Volunteers.

SUBJECT	PUPIL ACTIVITY
ENGLISH	Discussing, recording and presenting observations, experiences and opinions concerning the school grounds.
MATHEMATICS	Using the school grounds to explore the concepts of shape, space and size.
SCIENCE	Exploring the range of living things and materials present within the school grounds and identifying their properties. Exploring and observing the school grounds in terms of natural decay, seasonal changes and the effects of human activity.
TECHNOLOGY AND DESIGN	Designing and constructing artefacts to improve the school grounds, taking into account factors, such as cost, safety and suitable materials. Evaluating effectiveness.
HISTORY	Developing observation and skills of enquiry.
GEOGRAPHY	Using simple maps of the school area. Observing and enquiring into aspects of the physical environment of the school, for example, weather, vegetation, soils, animals and birds. Examining possible conflicts over the use of resources in the school grounds, for example, litter.
PHYSICAL EDUCATION	Placing and using equipment safely within the school grounds.
ART AND DESIGN	Recording sensory experiences and observations of the natural and made school environment. Designing and making images and objects based on observations.
MUSIC	Using sights and sounds of the school grounds as a stimulus for the composition of short pieces of music.
RELIGIOUS EDUCATION	Exploring God's role as creator and carer. Suggesting ways in which resources in the school grounds can be cared for and conserved.

LINKS WITH PROGRAMMES OF STUDY/ATTAINMENT TARGETS	LINKS WITH CROSS-CURRICULAR THEMES
• Talking and Listening • Writing	Cultural heritage Health education Information Technology
• Shape and Space • Measures	Information technology
• Living Things • Materials • Environment	Education for mutual understanding
• Social and Environmental Factors • Safety • Designing • Materials and Components	Health education
• Acquiring and Evaluating Historical Information	Cultural Heritage Education for mutual understanding
• Geographical Enquiry • Physical Environments • Issues in a Changing World	Health education Information technology
• Performance	Health education
• Investigating • Realising	Cultural heritage Information technology
• Making Music	Cultural heritage
• The Revelation of God • Morality	Cultural heritage Health education Education for mutual understanding

MAP 1

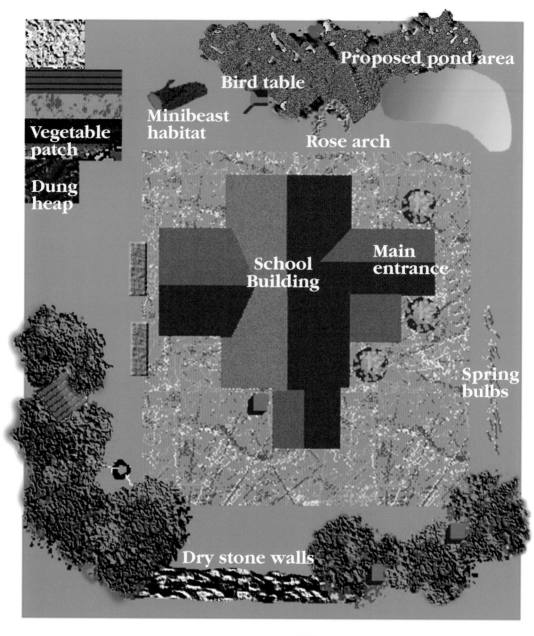

Proposed pond area

Bird table

Minibeast habitat

Vegetable patch

Dung heap

Rose arch

School Building

Main entrance

Spring bulbs

Dry stone walls

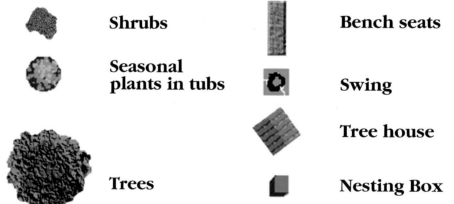

Shrubs

Bench seats

Seasonal plants in tubs

Swing

Trees

Tree house

Nesting Box

TABLE 2
TIMETABLE

ACTION	TARGET DATE
• Prepare an area for a compost heap, using logs as a surround.	March/April
• Prepare a vegetable patch and plant potatoes, peas, broad beans and cabbages.	May
• Arrange delivery of rotted manure.	June
• Plant bedding plants in wooden tubs.	June
• Create a mini-beast habitat near the compost heap.	September/October
• Construct and site a low-level treehouse/bird hide in the sheltered tree area.	October
• Hang a swing between two mature trees.	November
• Plant spring bulbs–snowdrops, daffodils, crocuses.	November
• Site nesting boxes/bird tables to allow their naturalisation before birds visit in the spring.	November/December
• Build a dry stone wall.	January/February
• Site bench seats.	February/March
• Establish a pond area.	March–ongoing

SCHOOL B:

A large special school catering for physically disabled pupils with academic abilities ranging from moderate learning difficulties to above average ability

DESIGNING A NATURE TRAIL FOR USE AS AN OUTDOOR CLASSROOM

The development of environmental education in our school began as an initiative which sought to provide stimuli for pupils with disabilities. We began in a small way, through using the school grounds as an outdoor classroom. This generated considerable enthusiasm amongst the pupils. It was also obvious that the school grounds offered considerable potential for developing the study of a variety of habitats. It seemed that the development of a Nature Trail would be an ideal way of utilising all the elements that the school site had to offer. The Trail would also provide a learning context for work in science, geography and art, a focus for creative writing and a stimulus for the communication of thoughts and feelings.

The Nature Trail took shape slowly over a period of six years. As the teacher with responsibility for the Special Programmes Department, I wanted to build on the work that other teachers had begun. The Trail is now used by pupils throughout the school as part of environmental education provision. The sketch of the Trail (see Map 2) highlights the features used for teaching and learning. The stages and groups involved in its development are included in Table 3. The Trail has facilitated project work in the following areas:

♦ pond dipping;

♦ bark rubbings;

♦ population studies, involving use of quadrats;

♦ fungus, leaf and flower identification and pressing;

♦ soil analysis;

♦ the use of information technology (IT) sensors;

♦ making casts of animal footprints.

Having an easily accessible area with so many different environments extends the number of practical activities that our pupils can experience. To be out and about, to see and to do, to use the senses, is an important process for our pupils. They experience a sense of achievement from practical environmental work which they may not achieve so readily from other curricular activities.

The use and maintenance of the Trail is regarded as an integral part of the life of the school and has proved an invaluable context for work across a range of subjects. Table 4 sets out examples of environmental activities carried out by pupils using the Nature Trail which can be linked to the subject requirements of the curriculum.

Throughout the development of the Nature Trail we entered, and were successful in, competitions organised by the Ulster Wildlife Trust, Conservation Volunteers, The Wildfowl and Wetlands Trust and the Royal Anniversary Trust. We used the prize money to purchase plants and carry out further improvements. A Department of Environment grant allowed us to purchase the rubber lining for the pond. The school is also a member of the WATCH club organised by the Ulster Wildlife Trust and the Young Ornithologists Club run by the Royal Society for the Protection of Birds. The Nature Trail provides the context for associated activities.

The development and use of the Nature Trail in the school has enabled the pupils to develop a sense of ownership and stewardship for the environment and to see it as a whole-school issue rather than the preserve of individual subjects. It is hoped that, over the next few years, the momentum of our present efforts will be sustained. We are currently investigating methods by which we can make the trail accessible to community groups and other schools. We are seeking a balance between allowing interested groups access to the Trail and maintaining our responsibility for its preservation. Pupils are learning to deal with one of the major dilemmas facing conservationists!

Note: Schools planning to develop their school grounds as a context for learning about the environment may find the following two references particularly useful.

REFERENCES

Learning Through Landscapes: Using School Grounds as an Educational Resource, K Young, 1990. Winchester: Learning Through Landscapes Trust.

Practical Conservation Pack: Advice for Teachers, Compiled by Conservation Volunteers/Shell Better Britain on behalf of the Ulster Tree Committee, 1987. Belfast: Conservation Volunteers.

MAP2

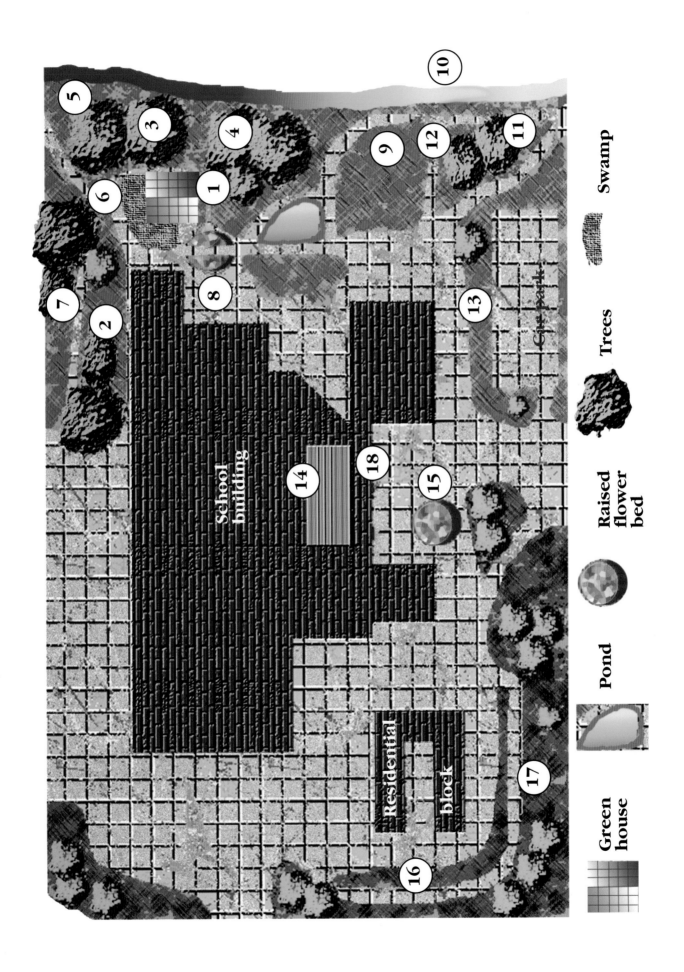

Swamp

Trees

Raised flower bed

Pond

Green house

23

KEY FOR NATURE TRAIL

1	Greenhouses	Indoor plants cultivated and seedlings raised.
2	Rockery	Plants typical to rockeries.
3	Herb bed	Nine varieties of herbs used in cooking.
4	Harrison Way	Some exotic trees.
5	Meadow	Fields not cut regularly (grasses and wild flowers).
6	The 'Swamp'	An area of poor drainage. A home for pond animals.
7	Copse	A variety of trees.
8	Bird garden	A number of different mini-habitats.
9	Hedgerow trail	Birds, wild plants and insects.
10	Stream	A damp and shady habitat.
11	The 'Glade'	A habitat for plants and insects which like shade.
12	Butterfly garden	Bright scented flowers which attract insects.
13	'Old House Lawns'	Exotic and native plants.
14	Poultry unit	Different breeds of bantam.
15	Special Units Garden	Indigenous wildflowers grown from seed.
16	Woodlands trail	Woodland habitat.
17	Woodlands	Deciduous trees.
18	Display Centre	Widllife display.

TABLE 3
STAGES IN THE DEVELOPMENT OF THE NATURE TRAIL

YEAR	DEVELOPMENT UNDERTAKEN	GROUPS INVOLVED IN PROJECT
1985	Copse	Senior School pupils, supported by the Ulster Society for the Preservation of the Countryside; Ministry of Agriculture, Forestry Division.
1986	Rockery	Senior School pupils, supported by a group of young people on a Youth Training Programme.
1987	Swamp	Senior School pupils, with advice and maintenance provided by Belfast Education and Library Board.
1988	Hedgerow trail	Senior School pupils, supported by a group of young people on a Youth Training Programme, and Conservation Volunteers.
	Butterfly garden	The School Scout group, supported by Conservation Volunteers.
	Glade	A group of young people on a Youth Training Programme.
	Poultry unit	Pupils from the Special Programmes Department with funding from 'Children in Need', 'Telethon', and practical help from the Northern Ireland Association for the Care and Resettlement of Offenders.
1989	Woodland trail	Senior School pupils, supported by Conservation Volunteers and advice and maintenance from Belfast Education and Library Board.
1990	Bird garden and meadow	Special Programmes Department.
1991	Stream	Advice and maintenance from Belfast Education and Library Board; the Water Division of the Department of Environment; and Ulster Wildlife Trust.
	Butterfly bank	Senior School pupils, Special Programmes Department, supported by Association of Landscape Contractors of Ireland.
	Nature Trail booklet and signs	Science Department, Special Programmes Department.

TABLE 4

SUBJECT	PUPIL ACTIVITY	LINKS WITH PROGRAMMES OF STUDY/ATTAINMENT TARGETS	LINKS WITH CROSS-CURRICULAR THEMES
ENGLISH	Sensory stimulation provides material for discussion. Interacting with others, exploring ideas and discussing issues. Observing and giving descriptions. Participating in activities which involve talking with others in the community.	• Talking and Listening • Writing	Information technology
MATHEMATICS	Counting. Sorting and pairing. Time and seasons. Making measurements and understanding size and shape. Data collection and handling.	• Number • Handling Data • Shape and Space • Measures	Information technology
SCIENCE	Identifying plants and animals. Learning what plants and animals need to sustain life. Discovering the ecological principles on which living things depend. Developing skills of scientific investigation. Observing decay and change of materials over time.	• Exploring and Investigating in Science • Living Things • Materials • Environment	Education for mutual understanding Information technology

GEOGRAPHY	Continuous surveying of the stream. Studying the effects of human activity on the environment. Recording seasonal weather changes. Studying the influences on soil and vegetation. Making plans and maps. Examining conflicts over the use of resources in the school grounds.	• Geographical Enquiry • Physical Environments • Issues in a Changing World	Education for mutual understanding Information technology
TECHNOLOGY AND DESIGN	Selecting materials and designing, for example, pond, raised beds.	• Designing • Materials and Components	Health education
HISTORY	Understanding the concept of time.	• Knowledge and Understanding of History	
ART AND DESIGN	Recording sensory experiences and observations of the school environment in collage and wall hangings. Designing scrapbooks for competitions. Making puppets to represent living things.	• Investigating • Realising	
RELIGIOUS EDUCATION	Fostering awareness and feeling for the created world. Discovering ways to care for the environment, both individually and as a school.	• The Revelation of God • Morality	

SCHOOL C:
A large co-educational post-primary school

RAISING AWARENESS OF ENVIRONMENTAL ISSUES IN THE SCHOOL, THE HOME AND THE COMMUNITY

The idea of 'taking action' for the environment was put forward by a number of pupils in Year 11. Stimulated by issues concerning the environment which were raised in a range of subjects and also by media coverage, pupils approached the Vice-principal with the suggestion that the school could be more environmentally friendly.

The pupils pointed out also that more could be done in their homes to support and care for the environment and suggested that care for the environment should be a priority issue in the school.

After discussions, it was agreed that a useful starting point would be for pupils to carry out an environmental audit in the school and in their homes and, on the basis of the outcomes and recommendations, a school policy would be developed to take account of environmental issues.

The Vice-principal discussed the idea with the whole staff and asked four departments (English, geography, home economics and science) to co-ordinate the work of pupils and, where possible, to link it with ongoing curricular work. A suggestion was made by some staff that an audit of the local community might be also a useful way of raising awareness and providing opportunities for pupils to engage in environmental improvement.

Heads of department agreed that all classes in Year 11 would be involved. Departments took responsibility for various activities. Questionnaires were devised during English classes and then forwarded to the geography, home economics and science departments for pupils to plan, organise and conduct the surveys. When the data had been collected, pupils designed a database to facilitate continuous evaluation and monitoring. In geography, home economics and science classes, pupils analysed the data and drew up their recommendations.

A sample of the questionnaire designed to carry out the environmental audit in the school is included in Table 5. A sample of the questionnaire which was taken home and completed by pupils is included in Table 6. A schedule of the activities carried out by pupils in the local community is included in Table 7.

It took most of two terms, from the time the initial idea emerged, until the recommendations for improvement were drawn up by pupils. These recommendations are as follows:

The school

♦ Find a suitable place in school to store waste paper and aluminium cans for recycling.

♦ Investigate litter production and distribution, in order to re-locate litter bins, both inside school and in the grounds.

♦ Form a young naturalists' club which would meet after school once a week and organise outings, such as bird watching, beach combing, fishing trips and rambles.

♦ Improve the school grounds by tree planting, adding nesting boxes and leaving part of the grounds unmown to encourage the growth of wild plants.

♦ Adjust the heating boiler daily to take account of changes in the weather.

- Fit thermostats to radiators so that south-facing classrooms are not excessively heated.

- Encourage pupils and staff to use alternative forms of transport, such as bicycles, public transport or walking.

The home

- Sort household waste into organic, plastic, aluminium and glass for recycling.

- Use low-energy lightbulbs.

- Insulate roofspace, doors and windows.

- Install room thermostats.

- Purchase recycled paper products, where possible.

- Purchase environmentally friendly cleaning materials.

- Avoid the purchase of aerosols containing chlorofluorocarbons.

- Use unleaded petrol in cars.

The community

- Plant trees in key areas throughout the town.

- Encourage local supermarkets to establish bottle banks to recycle glass.

- Campaign among local farmers and local factories to treat chemical waste before it is discharged into the river.

- Highlight litter 'hot spots' and seek more bins from local district council for those areas, for example, near carry-out cafés.

- Discuss, with the local police, ways to improve traffic congestion in the town.

- Volunteer to clean up a derelict area of public ground close to the school.

The outcomes of the three surveys and the recommendations were displayed in the school foyer. In addition, letters enclosing the findings and recommendations of the survey were sent to parents and to key people in the community including the local Member of Parliament. Staff discussed the findings and recommendations on a day of exceptional closure and a small working group was set up to develop a whole-school policy for environmental education which would take account of pupils' views.

TABLE 5
PART 1 SURVEY QUESTIONS FOR ENVIRONMENTAL AUDIT OF SCHOOL

CATEGORY	ISSUES	YES	SOME-TIMES	NO
1 USE OF ENERGY	Is the amount of electricity used during the last school year greater than the previous year?			
	Is the amount of oil used during the last school year greater than the previous year?			
	Are thermostats fitted to radiators?			
	Are low energy lightbulbs used?			
	Does the school minibus run on unleaded petrol?			
	Are outside doors and windows insulated?			

Any relevant comments

_____

_____

_____

CATEGORY	ISSUES	YES	SOME-TIMES	NO
2 MANAGEMENT OF WASTE	Does the school collect for recycling:			
	• waste paper?			
	• aluminium cans?			
	• glass?			
	Is canteen waste recycled?			
	Are litter bins adequate?			
	Is litter obvious:			
	• in desks?			
	• behind radiators?			
	• on corridors?			
	Is there plastic rubbish in the bins?			

Any relevant comments

_____

_____

_____

CATEGORY	ISSUES	YES	SOME-TIMES	NO
3 USE OF MATERIAL	Is the paper in printers used efficiently?			
	Are disposable cups and plates used?			
	Is the complete use of notebooks and file pages encouraged?			

Any relevant comments

_____

_____

_____

TABLE 5 continued

CATEGORY	ISSUES	YES	SOME-TIMES	NO
4 PURCHASE OF MATERIALS	Is the amount of paper used for photocopying in the last school year greater than the previous year?			
	Does the school buy recycled paper products?			
	Are the cleaning materials environmentally friendly?			
	Does the canteen buy organically grown foods?			

Any relevant comments

_____

_____

_____

CATEGORY	ISSUES	YES	SOME-TIMES	NO
5 ATTITUDES OF STAFF AND PUPILS	Do staff and pupils generally switch off lights when not in use?			
	Are outside doors always kept closed?			
	Is the environment ever a topic for school assembly?			
	Is there a wildlife club in school?			
	Has the school entered any environmental competitions in the last year?			
	Has the school in the last year taken part in any environmental events, such as Tree Week?			

Any relevant comments

_____

_____

_____

PART 2 SURVEY QUESTIONS FOR ENVIRONMENTAL AUDIT OF SCHOOL: SCHOOL GROUNDS

6 What do you think are a visitor's first impressions when entering the school grounds? ———————

———

What specific aspects do you think need to be improved? ———————————————

———

7 Which school subjects use the school grounds as part of formal lessons? ———————————

———

8 What extra-curricular activities take place in the school grounds? ———————————————

———

9 What happens to grass cuttings and hedge clippings? ———————————————————

———

10 Which of the following exist in the school grounds?

	YES	NO
seat		
play equipment		
hedges		
fences or walls		
bird table		
pond or stream		
trees or wood		

	YES	NO
nesting boxes		
greenhouse		
compost heat		
weather station		
nature trail		
mown grass		
'wild' area		

11 Are there signs of graffiti or vandalism and, if so, where are they concentrated? ———————

———

12 Is litter obvious in the grounds? ———————————————————————————————

Where does it collect most? ———————————————————————————————

At what times of day is it most obvious? ———————————————————————

13 Which of the following flora and fauna are present in the school grounds:

	YES	NO
conifers, for example, pine and fir		
deciduous trees, for example, ash, beach and rowan		
evergreens, for example, holly		
shrubs, for example, broom, escalonia and laurel		
butterflies		
bats		
wild birds, for example, robins and sparrows		
small mammals, for example, squirrels and field mice		
trees or wood		
wildflowers, for example, buttercups, bluebells and vetch		

TABLE 6
SURVEY QUESTIONS FOR ENVIRONMENTAL AUDIT OF THE HOME

CATEGORY	ISSUES	YES	SOME-TIMES	NO
1 USE OF ENERGY	Is the amount of electricity used during the last year greater than the previous year?			
	Is the amount of oil, gas or coal used during last year greater than the previous year?			
	Are thermostats fitted to radiators?			
	Are low energy lightbulbs used?			
	If you have a car, does it run on unleaded petrol?			
	Are outside doors and windows insulated?			

Any relevant comments

_____

_____

_____

CATEGORY	ISSUES	YES	SOME-TIMES	NO
2 MANAGEMENT OF WASTE	Does the family collect waste for recycling purposes:			
	• waste paper?			
	• aluminium cans?			
	• glass?			
	Is kitchen waste recycled?			
	Are newspapers and magazines recycled?			
	Is garden waste used for compost?			
	Is the garden sprayed with fertilisers or pesticides?			

Any relevant comments

_____

_____

_____

CATEGORY	ISSUES	YES	SOME-TIMES	NO
3 SHOPPING	Does the family buy recycled paper products?			
	Are the household cleaning materials environmentally friendly?			
	Does the family buy organically grown foods?			

Any relevant comments

_____

_____

_____

TABLE 6 continued

CATEGORY	ISSUES	YES	SOME-TIMES	NO
5 ATTITUDES OF FAMILY MEMBERS	Does the family generally switch off lights when not in use?			
	On family outings, is rubbish disposed of carefully or taken home?			
	Does the family visit outdoor recreation areas, such as forests and country parks?			
	Has any family member ever taken part in a local environmental issue or project?			
	Do family members take part in outdoor leisure activities, such as bird watching, fishing or hillwalking?			

Any relevant comments

_____

_____

_____

TABLE 7
ENVIRONMENTAL SURVEY IN THE LOCAL COMMUNITY

CATEGORY	ACTIVITIES OF PUPILS
ENVIRONMENTAL QUALITY	Shading on Ordnance Survey map of the local area to highlight three categories of environmental quality: • good; • average; • poor.
WATER PROVISION AND QUALITY	Testing rivers for pollution using the National River Watch Testing Kit.
AIR QUALITY	Observing and recording smoke, fumes, farm slurry, dust, industrial and vehicle emissions.
WASTE DISPOSAL	Assessing methods of waste collection. Litter survey to identify problem areas and times when production occurred.
ENERGY	Surveying, at random, households to determine main energy sources, consumption levels and efficiency measures taken.
NOISE POLLUTION	Surveying, at random, noise levels under a range of categories, such as traffic, domestic, industrial, entertainment and leisure.
CONSERVATION AREAS	Surveying and recording, for example, listed buildings, ancient monuments, parks, wildlife areas.
WILDLIFE SURVEY	Surveying wildlife species. Assessing and documenting habitats.
TRANSPORT	Surveying the volume of local traffic and assessing problems.

PART B:
A RANGE OF APPROACHES TO ENVIRONMENTAL WORK IN SCHOOLS

INTRODUCTION

These exemplars highlight the use of facilities provided by a variety of statutory and voluntary bodies, such as countryside centres, forest parks and residential centres; involvement in national and international projects; joint work in the environment as part of education for mutual understanding (EMU) programmes; and inter-departmental projects. They illustrate how environmental activities can be integrated readily into the curriculum.

EXEMPLAR 1

USING THE ENVIRONMENT AS A CONTEXT FOR EDUCATION FOR MUTUAL UNDERSTANDING–THE SPEEDWELL PROJECT

Two local primary schools decided to use the environment as a context for their joint education for mutual understanding programme. Teachers contacted the director of the 'Speedwell' Project based in Parkanaur Forest in the Southern Education and Library Board area.

A meeting was arranged and the director explained that the object of the 'Speedwell' project was to encourage pupils to:

♦ study the environment from a variety of perspectives;

♦ examine natural woodland, lakes and rivers, taking account of biological, historical, aesthetic and geographical aspects;

♦ carry out work with another school to exchange information and views.

The teachers and director planned a programme to suit the needs of the pupils, taking account of time constraints, volume of work and the need to set realistic targets.

The programme outline included:

♦ following the Speedwell Nature Trail workbook to study wildlife;

♦ a 'look, listen, touch and tell' session which concentrated on sensory stimuli;

♦ a study of the history of the area by observation, including the consideration of the age of trees and architecture of buildings;

♦ a follow-up session back in the schools, involving artwork and making a Victorian newspaper page to describe the environment at that time;

♦ visiting each other's school to observe displays of work;

♦ a follow-up session at Peatlands Park, Loughgall, where pupils engaged in an aquatic study, involving pond dipping and exercises related to the habitat of peatlands.

Teachers in both schools found that the project helped pupils learn about and enjoy different environments, heightened their awareness of the complexities of environment studied, and acted as a catalyst for them to develop similar studies in other habitats.

EXEMPLAR 2

EARTH EDUCATION

Pupils at Key Stage 2 in this primary school had carried out some work on the environment in the first term. The teacher wanted to reinforce and consolidate their learning by introducing sensory and conceptual experiences. The teacher contacted the Warden at the Kilbroney Conservation Centre in the Southern Education and Library Board area to arrange a one-day visit to the centre as part of the 'Earth Caretakers' programme. She describes the experience as follows:

Once we agreed to take part in the programme, the activities started in the classroom two or three weeks before the visit. The class received a slightly battered box containing a small dustbin and a riddle which encouraged the children to analyse waste and the reasons why species are endangered. The dustbin contained an environmental action pack to introduce the class to the concepts of energy flow, food webs, chemical cycles and how everything changes with time. The pupils were also invited to take part in an experiential activity on the visit to the field centre.

The day at the centre was a great adventure, designed to help young people become caretakers of the earth and its life. Through experiencing, touching, smelling, seeing and listening, the children learnt five secrets about planet earth and, at the end of the day, learnt the answer to the riddle.

The 'Earth Caretakers' programme seeks to engage pupils in activities that enable them to understand how energy and materials tie all life together. They can experience the natural world positively and undertake personal lifestyle changes in school and at home, all with a view to understanding and caring for the environment. In turn, they may be able to help others have more feeling for, and understanding of, the earth and its life. Pupils' evaluative comments showed that they found learning about the environment fun.

EXEMPLAR 3

ASSESSING THE IMPACT OF URBAN AND INDUSTRIAL DEVELOPMENT ON THE ENVIRONMENT

The European Action for the Environment Project is part of a wider Organisation for Economic Co-operation and Development (OECD) environmental initiative. This is a cross-community and cross-border initiative involving schools from the north and south of Ireland. Year 10 pupils from two schools in Northern Ireland paired with their counterparts in the Republic to investigate their urban environments and to compare findings. Two of the schools studied the historical background of their areas, with residentials taking place in both Bangor and Dublin. The other two schools looked at the geographical aspects of their surroundings, with exchanges taking place between Belfast and Cork, and with each school hosting their partners while the studies were carried out.

The environmental work which the pupils carried out included:

♦ a local history study of a Victorian street;

♦ outlining the processes of urban landscape development;

♦ the management of an urban environment;

♦ the assessment of landscape quality;

♦ relating environmental factors to human well-being;

♦ observing the effects of air pollution on buildings;

♦ discussing the impact of tourism on the environment;

♦ monitoring traffic congestion and its effects.

For the pupils in Northern Ireland schools, this work fulfilled some of the requirements for the Programme of Study for Geography for Key Stage 3.

As a result of their work, the pupils identified present day environmental issues and suggested improvements. Valuable lessons were learned as they outlined courses of action needed to implement the improvements.

EXEMPLAR 4

DEVELOPING AN URBAN TRAIL TO STUDY THE BUILT ENVIRONMENT

This trail was developed by a teacher in a primary school in a large town. The local environment did not suggest immediately that there was scope for interesting environmental education, but the teacher wanted to highlight, for pupils, that the built environment was as important as the natural environment in terms of its vulnerability to human activity. The trail was developed with the assistance of an advisory teacher in the local Education and Library Board and is now an integral part of the school's environmental education programme.

The table opposite identifies key features on the trail, associated fieldwork activities and follow-up work back in the classroom. Each section is free–standing in order to take account of time constraints and allows pupils the opportunity to concentrate, in detail, on aspects of their local area.

URBAN TRAIL

When the pupils completed the urban trail, the teacher organised a field trip to a rural site so that pupils could experience different environments. Pupils visited the Ulster Wildlife Trust site at Crossgar where the theme 'Disappearing Habitats' is used to allow pupils to experience peatland, wetland, woodland and meadow habitats.

Environmental activities carried out by pupils on the urban trail and the visit to Crossgar have been successful in raising pupils' awareness to the environment which surrounds them and has increased their understanding of the part they can play in caring for their local environment. Pupils are more aware also that maintaining the balance of the global environment depends on them taking responsibility for their local environment.

FEATURES ON THE TRAIL	FIELDWORK ACTIVITIES	FOLLOW-UP IN CLASSROOM
THE HOTEL	Using grounds to study trees, wildlife and architecture of the building.	Investigate the effects of the built environment on the natural environment.
THE BRIDGE	Observing the work of the river– volume, speed, silt content, cleanliness.	Consider the effects of the growth of the town on the course of the river.
HEALTH CENTRE	Interviews with staff to discuss the environmental effects on health.	Consider the responsibilities with regard to health care and the importance of environmental factors.
THE RIVER BANK	Habitat studies. Monitoring of river pollution.	Investigate the effects of pollution on the river and flora and fauna living on the river bank.
MAIN STREET	A traffic survey, noting the volume of traffic, noise and air pollution.	Consider and investigate the issue of traffic pollution leading to an understanding of global warming and the greenhouse effect, linking local issues to global issues.
THE SUPERMARKET	A survey of renewable resources based on a study of materials used in packaging.	Investigate the way in which glass, paper and cans can be recycled. Pupils encouraged to devise plans for recycling at home and school.
HIGH STREET	An urban land use survey, noting the use of each building under headings: • commercial; • residential; • public building. Noting environmental quality under the headings: • good; • satisfactory; • poor.	Investigate and consider environmental quality, noting areas which were unacceptable and identifying issues, such as vandalism.

EXEMPLAR 5

ENVIRONMENTAL STUDY OF A LOCAL RIVERBANK

The science and geography departments of this post-primary school decided to carry out joint fieldwork with Key Stage 3 pupils linked to their respective programmes of study.

Teachers identified the curriculum content which could be taught through organised fieldwork exercises. They developed workbooks and activity worksheets for all pupils throughout Key Stage 3.

Half-day visits to selected sites were organised three times a year for each year group.

The table below lists the environmental activities carried out by pupils. Teachers selected, from the table, the combination of activities which was appropriate to any particular visit and which linked with ongoing work in the classroom.

The two departments have found the joint planning, co-ordination and organisation of fieldwork activities invaluable in terms of developing team teaching; avoiding duplication of activities; helping pupils to make connections across subject boundaries; and facilitating the logistics of planning fieldwork.

FIELDWORK SITE	ENVIRONMENTAL ACTIVITIES CARRIED OUT
THE RIVER	• surveying water speed, depth of channel, variations of stream flow • observing evidence of erosion and deposition • identifying pollution and its source • identifying uses of the river • analysing flooding–causes and effects • carrying out mapwork and contour exercises • assessing the human impact on the river
THE RIVER BANK	• identifying flora and fauna • studying flower and plant structure • making transect studies at different sites • recording evidence of wildlife on the river bank • recording the micro-climate • studying the relationships between plants and animals in their habitat • comparing soil tests at different distances from river • using a National River Watch Pack
THE MIXED WOODLAND	• making tree studies–identifying species, numbers and ages • measuring growth over time • observing seasonal changes • comparing, for example, evergreen/deciduous and hardwood/softwood • studying seeds and seedlings • analysing bark • studying parasitic relationships

EXEMPLAR 6

RESIDENTIAL FIELD TRIP

The teachers of the Year 7 classes in a large primary school had planned a number of units of work on the environment for the second term. They had also decided to organise a residential experience in Term 3 in one of the Education and Library Board field centres. It was hoped that this experience would reinforce and consolidate work completed by pupils in Term 2 and would provide a social opportunity for teachers and pupils before the pupils transferred to their new school.

The Year 7 pupils had a three day visit during which four outdoor sessions were organised. These are described in the table below.

ACTIVITIES AT THE FIELD CENTRE

Teachers and pupils found the residential provided valuable and enjoyable first-hand experience of a variety of habitats. They also appreciated the other advantages which the centre had to offer, such as:

- the provision of waterproof clothing and equipment;
- the local expertise to help with teaching;
- transport and access to safe suitable fieldwork sites;
- opportunities for social and personal development.

Note: The field centre can be used as part of an induction programme for pupils in Year 8. At Key Stage 2 or 3 teachers may wish to utilise, to the full, the experience and expertise of the centre staff to suggest and lead activities. On the other hand, some A-level students may wish to use the facilities and equipment of the centre to carry out their own investigations.

SESSIONS	ENVIRONMENTAL ACTIVITIES
A BEACH STUDY	• comparing rocky and sandy habitats and shore-life • observing life in rock pools • observing tidal changes and the movement of sand and pebbles along the shore • identifying plants and animals along a transect from high to low water mark
A RIVER STUDY	• measuring river speed, depth and width • observing pebble shapes and sizes • discussing the issue of litter and pollution
A FOREST WALK	• identifying trees and distinguishing conifers, broadleaves and evergreens • making a night safari to identify nocturnal animals and finding direction using the stars • observing forest industries • discussing the issue of conflict between forestry, recreation, water supply and sheep farming on moorland
A MAPPING EXERCISE	• playing a compass game where pupils are given a list of directions to follow which will lead them back to the start • learning and applying land use classifications • orienteering

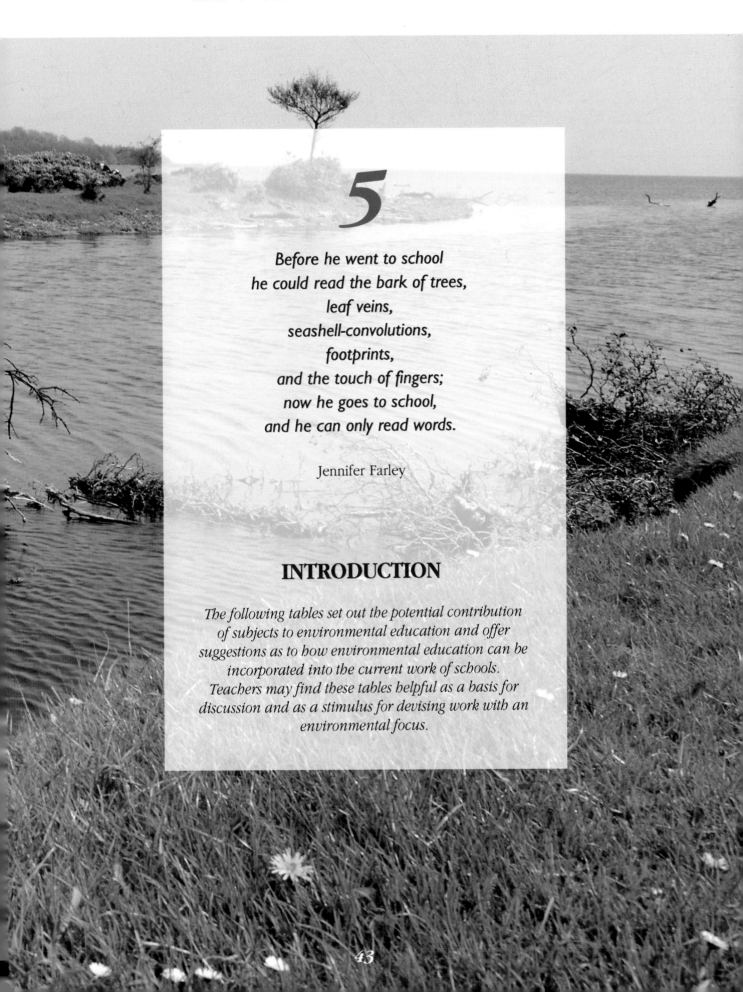

SUBJECT CONTRIBUTIONS TO ENVIRONMENTAL EDUCATION

5

*Before he went to school
he could read the bark of trees,
leaf veins,
seashell-convolutions,
footprints,
and the touch of fingers;
now he goes to school,
and he can only read words.*

Jennifer Farley

INTRODUCTION

*The following tables set out the potential contribution
of subjects to environmental education and offer
suggestions as to how environmental education can be
incorporated into the current work of schools.
Teachers may find these tables helpful as a basis for
discussion and as a stimulus for devising work with an
environmental focus.*

KEY STAGE 2

THE POTENTIAL CONTRIBUTION OF SUBJECTS AT KEY STAGES 1 AND 2 TO ENVIRONMENTAL EDUCATION

ENGLISH

Key Stage 1

KEY STAGE 1

Teachers could explore the environmental dimension by providing pupils with opportunities to:

◆ engage in talking and listening, reading and writing about some of the shared features of everyday life in Northern Ireland to develop appreciation of their environment.

POSSIBLE ACTIVITIES

Pupils might be provided with opportunities for talking and listening, reading and writing about some of the shared features of everyday life in Northern Ireland, for example, 'our' street, the park, the river, the hill; thereby developing a knowledge and appreciation of their immediate environment.

Key Stage 2

Teachers could explore the environmental dimension by providing pupils with opportunities to:

◆ interact with their teacher, other pupils and adult visitors and might include visits outside the classroom to interesting places and other schools;

◆ consider their experiences of their own home environment and family structures and how these compare with the experiences of others in the past, now and in other parts of the world.

POSSIBLE ACTIVITIES

Pupils might read, discuss and write about the environment, describing nature, the seasons, the weather and its effects, or an aspect of pollution, such as the effect of an oil spillage on birds. Pupils might visit interesting places in the environment, such as the Silent Valley, the Giant's Causeway, a farm, a cleansing depot or a local factory. Preparatory and follow-up work might focus on talking and listening, reading and writing activities, describing responses to different environments.

44

THE POTENTIAL CONTRIBUTION OF SUBJECTS AT KEY STAGES 1 AND 2 TO ENVIRONMENTAL EDUCATION

MATHEMATICS

Teachers could explore the environmental dimension by providing pupils with opportunities to:

♦ explore and handle a wide variety of materials including natural, made and scrap materials;

♦ observe themselves and their environment to develop ideas of shape and space.

POSSIBLE ACTIVITIES

Pupils could look at and discuss shapes that occur in natural materials, such as pebbles, shells, fir cones and shapes that occur in the natural world, such as honeycomb, rings on bark of trees, various shapes of leaves. Pupils could classify materials according to whether they are made or natural and begin to appreciate those materials found in the environment.

Teachers could explore the environmental dimension by providing pupils with opportunities to:

♦ extend their appreciation of position, movement and direction in space, by exploring their environment at first-hand;

♦ use a wide variety of materials and tools to develop their mathematical skills and concepts;

♦ discuss, describe, compare and explain all aspects of their mathematics work.

POSSIBLE ACTIVITIES

Pupils might have opportunities to discuss shapes found in nature, such as honeycomb, rings on bark of trees, various leaf shapes, symmetry in nature, such as the pine cone, butterfly wings.

SCIENCE

KEY STAGE 2

Teachers could explore the environmental dimension by providing pupils with opportunities to:

- sort living things into groups using observable features, for example, animals which have fur, feathers, scales;

- explore and investigate a local habitat and the plants and animals that live there;

- develop an awareness and understanding of the necessity for sensitive collection of living things in studies of the environment;

- appreciate the need to conserve the natural environment;

- investigate and measure similarities and differences among plants and animals;

- develop skills in identifying locally occurring species of animals and plants by observing external features and using simple keys;

- discuss the use of colour in the natural environment, for example, camouflage, attraction of insects to flowers, warning signs;

- observe and explore some ways in which plant and animal behaviour is influenced by environmental conditions, including seasonal and daily changes;

- be aware of the existence of past life forms, such as the sabre-toothed tiger and the woolly mammoth;

- recognise that human activities can influence the environment and can contribute to the extinction of plant and animal life forms;

- order living things in a food chain, such as grass, rabbit, fox.

POSSIBLE ACTIVITIES

Pupils might classify rubbish into groups, for example, according to the material from which it was made. Pupils could be involved in an environmental clean-up campaign or could visit a local Council rubbish tip.

KEY STAGE 1

Teachers could explore the environmental dimension by providing pupils with opportunities to:

- find out about the variety of animal and plant life both through direct observations and by using secondary sources, such as books, stories, pictures, charts and videos;

- observe and gain an awareness of living things in their local environment;

- investigate similarities and differences among plants and animals in their local environment;

- sort living things into groups using observable features, for example, animals which have fur, feathers, scales;

- observe seasonal changes and how these affect plants and animals, for example, buds, and birds building nests;

- explore the range of litter in and around their own locality;

- investigate how human activities create a variety of waste products.

POSSIBLE ACTIVITIES

Groups of pupils might create their own mini-trail to be followed by other members of the class. Coloured pegs, or other similar devices, could be used to indicate particular points on the trail at which there was something to see, for example, where particular animals lived.

THE POTENTIAL CONTRIBUTION OF SUBJECTS AT KEY STAGES 1 AND 2 TO ENVIRONMENTAL EDUCATION

TECHNOLOGY AND DESIGN

Teachers could explore the environmental dimension by providing pupils with opportunities to:

◆ gain an awareness of the function of both natural and made objects in their environment and of the products they make;

◆ ask questions about natural and made objects in their immediate environment and products they have made, and to suggest practical changes that could be made in response to needs identified by themselves and others.

POSSIBLE ACTIVITIES

Pupils could be encouraged to talk about the nature and function of natural and made objects in their environment.

Teachers could explore the environmental dimension by providing pupils with opportunities to:

◆ become aware that technology and design activities often raise environmental issues which may need to be taken into consideration;

◆ appreciate the effects of these activities in everyday life, such as the use of plastic packaging;

◆ use their environment to identify opportunities for technology and design activities;

◆ investigate both familiar and unfamiliar situations in order to generate ideas and opportunities.

POSSIBLE ACTIVITIES

Pupils might consider the design of bridges and the impact of these bridges on the environment, as part of a project on bridges.

THE POTENTIAL CONTRIBUTION OF SUBJECTS AT KEY STAGES 1 AND 2 TO ENVIRONMENTAL EDUCATION

GEOGRAPHY

KEY STAGE 2

Teachers could explore the environmental dimension by providing pupils with opportunities to:

◆ learn about a variety of typical environments of the earth, the physical and human processes which contribute to them and some of the issues arising;

◆ collect and record information gained at first-hand through the observation of the local environment;

◆ recognise that people use renewable and non-renewable resources;

◆ identify features which illustrate differences between places, for example, town and countryside, coast and mountain;

◆ understand that plants, animals and birds are associated with physical conditions relating to their different habitats;

◆ identify simple relationships between the human and physical elements of landscapes by the study of contrasting areas of Northern Ireland;

◆ investigate issues which arise when individuals or groups have conflicting views on the use of resources, including the management of the environment. One issue should be environmental and one developmental, one at a local or regional scale and the other at a global scale.

POSSIBLE ACTIVITIES

Pupils might use secondary sources to see how animal and plant life is influenced by climate in the tropical rainforest or hot desert. They might compare the plant and animal life found in sunny/shady, windy/sheltered, wet/dry, conditions in the school grounds.

KEY STAGE 1

Teachers could explore the environmental dimension by providing pupils with opportunities to:

◆ identify similarities and differences in the environment and suggest simple relationships between the physical environment and human activities;

◆ understand that plants, animals and birds are associated with physical conditions relating to where they live and what they feed on;

◆ identify a variety of natural materials;

◆ identify simple features of the physical landscape, for example, hill, river, valley;

◆ identify, describe and record, in appropriate forms, some details of the natural physical features and those built by humans in their own neighbourhood;

◆ identify features which illustrate differences between town and country, coastal and mountainous areas;

◆ investigate at least one issue relating to the environment.

POSSIBLE ACTIVITIES

Pupils might be taken on a sensory walk of a local park and be encouraged to touch, smell, listen to and observe the environment. Pupils might talk about the effect of litter in the playground, street or local park and consider suggestions as to how the situation might be improved.

48

HISTORY

KEY STAGE 2

Teachers could explore the environmental dimension by providing pupils with opportunities to:

◆ study a School Designed Unit, involving the investigation of an aspect of the history of the locality, for example

• an aspect of the local community over a long period of time, such as, housing, schools, churches, or the development of a local building or site over a long period of time.

POSSIBLE ACTIVITIES

Pupils might be asked to identify historic aspects of the environment which have been preserved and those which have been lost and to consider how important aspects of the environment can be preserved. Pupils might consider the effects on the local environment of the changes which have taken place over time.

KEY STAGE 1

Teachers could explore the environmental dimension by providing pupils with opportunities to:

◆ use the local environment to develop their powers of observation and ask historical questions;

◆ focus on selected aspects of the environment, for example, a particular building;

◆ become involved, gradually, in more extended explorations of their environment through comparing, for example, buildings of different periods.

POSSIBLE ACTIVITIES

Pupils might look at pictures of the local environment and talk about how it has changed over time. They could talk about some of the positive and negative effects of changes to the environment over time.

THE POTENTIAL CONTRIBUTION OF SUBJECTS AT KEY STAGES 1 AND 2 TO ENVIRONMENTAL EDUCATION

ART AND DESIGN

Key Stage 2

Teachers could explore the environmental dimension by providing pupils with opportunities to:

- enrich their sensory experiences and develop aesthetic awareness;

- make use of visits;

- look at the local environment and talk to people;

- investigate and record, experimenting with and using a variety of media and methods, from first-hand experience of the natural and made environments;

- make images and objects, based on direct observations of the natural and made environments, and from memory and imagination.

POSSIBLE ACTIVITIES

Pupils might compare differences in the appearance of buildings in a street, such as banks, garages, hotels and fast-food outlets. They might consider how the street could be made more environmentally attractive before creating a picture or making models.

Teachers could explore the environmental dimension by providing pupils with opportunities to:

- look at the local environment and talk to people;

- explore and record their direct sensory experiences and observations of the natural and made environments, both at home and at school;

- identify, discuss and record examples of art, design and craft in their environment;

- make images and objects, based on direct observations of the natural and made environments, and from memory and imagination.

POSSIBLE ACTIVITIES

Pupils might look at and talk about shapes and designs in the natural and made environment of the school area before making a group collage.

THE POTENTIAL CONTRIBUTION OF SUBJECTS AT KEY STAGES 1 AND 2 TO ENVIRONMENTAL EDUCATION

MUSIC

Teachers could explore the environmental dimension by providing pupils with opportunities to:

♦ develop an awareness of music and sound as part of both the natural and made environment.

POSSIBLE ACTIVITIES

Pupils might focus their attention on particular sounds which they hear in their immediate environment in order to develop the skill of active listening, for example, sounds within the classroom and school as well as sounds arising from the natural and made environment. The music of birds, the sounds from the town are all part of an increasing environmental awareness. Pupils might imitate such sounds imaginatively and make sound effects using voices, body sounds and natural and made materials including musical instruments. Pupils could also listen to musical pieces which suggest, or have been stimulated by, particular environments, for example, the sea, storms, the wind.

Teachers could explore the environmental dimension by providing pupils with opportunities to:

♦ develop an awareness and understanding of music and sound as part of both the natural and made environment.

POSSIBLE ACTIVITIES

Pupils might listen to music and talk about how the environment may have inspired the composers of works, such as the *Hebrides Overture* by Mendelssohn, *Vltava* by Smetana, *La Mer* by Debussy or *An American in Paris* by Gershwin in order to develop an awareness of context in relation to the music they experience. Pupils might create their own music inspired by features of their local environment, such as a river, mountain or park. They could also focus on the concept of noise pollution in relation to their own environment.

PHYSICAL EDUCATION

KEY STAGE 1

Teachers could explore the environmental dimension by providing pupils with opportunities to:

◆ develop skills while exploring their school or locality;

◆ develop an awareness of basic safety practices;

◆ develop concepts of directionality by observation of weather lore and seasonal changes;

◆ develop positive attitudes towards the care of the environment.

POSSIBLE ACTIVITIES

Pupils could develop positive attitudes of care towards the environment keeping to paths, closing gates, not pulling plants or dropping litter during outdoor activities.

KEY STAGE 2

Teachers could explore the environmental dimension by providing pupils with opportunities to:

◆ develop skills in basic safety in different localities;

◆ develop observation and directional concepts in extended walks, orienteering courses and treasure hunts.

POSSIBLE ACTIVITIES

During outdoor activities in the park, forest, hills, seashore, pupils should observe safety codes and understand that they could damage the environment by using unauthorised routes, swinging on branches of trees, dropping litter or by lighting fires.

RELIGIOUS EDUCATION

KEY STAGE 2

Teachers could explore the environmental dimension by providing pupils with opportunities to:

- explore the wonder and variety of creation;

- discover and reflect on the achievements of human creativity;

- explore how humans misuse their creative power, for example, through vandalism, violence, crime, destruction of rainforests, wastage of food;

- learn respect for the environment;

- consider the respect due to creation and the gifts of God;

- discover the challenge for humans to become co-workers with God for a better world.

POSSIBLE ACTIVITIES

Pupils might make an illustrated leaflet on the local area, make a list of items which can be recycled, participate in a fund-raising project which will enable others to improve their environment, or design a poster reflecting the need to care for the environment.

KEY STAGE 1

Teachers could explore the environmental dimension by providing pupils with opportunities to:

- illustrate the wonder and variety of God's creation;

- talk about what God has made, people, flowers, birds, animals, plant bulbs and seeds;

- observe the way in which natural things grow, go for a nature walk, collect leaves, pine cones, make seasonal displays, look after birds and animals;

- develop respect for the environment;

- develop a caring attitude towards living things;

- realise that each person has a responsibility to care for the environment.

POSSIBLE ACTIVITIES

Pupils might talk about what God has made, such as people, flowers, birds, animals, plant bulbs and seeds. They might observe the way in which natural things grow; go for a nature walk and collect leaves, pine cones, of autumn fruits and vegetables. Pupils could make a class book depicting growing things and how they change. They could make a chart listing ways in which they can care for the world around them; keep their classroom and environment litter-free; plant seeds and bulbs; and care for animals.

THE POTENTIAL CONTRIBUTION OF SUBJECTS AT KEY STAGES 3 AND 4 TO ENVIRONMENTAL EDUCATION

ENGLISH

Teachers could explore the environmental dimension by providing pupils with opportunities to:

♦ discuss controversial issues, for example, environmental pollution and show awareness of sources of help and guidance.

POSSIBLE ACTIVITIES

Pupils might discuss, read and write about a range of issues relating to the environment including, for example, local, national and international pollution; the growth of the world's population; the depletion of national resources.

Teachers could explore the environmental dimension by providing pupils with opportunities to:

♦ plan, organise and participate with fluency in a group presentation or performance related to the protection of the environment;

♦ select and use information from appropriate sources to investigate a topic being studied, for example, a computer database may be used to access information for a project on local studies;

♦ demonstrate in talking and writing, an understanding of the perceived intentions of the author in texts they are reading or watching, for example, how information on an environmental or political issue is presented and consider instances of underlying bias or prejudice;

♦ make a selection, from a range of reference materials, and use their information management skills to identify key points, for example, research and present a project on pollution;

♦ produce pieces of writing structured effectively and appropriately for the purpose, for example, write a dialogue about a controversial environmental issue.

POSSIBLE ACTIVITIES

Pupils might have opportunities to research and debate environmental dilemmas, such as the siting of a new factory in an area of high unemployment which is also in a 'green belt', or a road improvement scheme which necessitates the filling in of part of a lake which is a home for wildlife.

Pupils might have opportunities to consider environmental issues in literature studied, in prose, such as *The Grapes of Wrath* by J Steinbeck, *The Power and the Glory* by G Greene; in poems, such as *Cynddylan on a Tractor* by R S Thomas; in drama, such as *The Field* by J B Keane, *The Plough and the Stars* and *Juno and the Paycock* by S O'Casey.

MATHEMATICS

Teachers could explore the environmental dimension by providing pupils with opportunities to:

◆ develop mathematical processes through practical tasks, real-life problems and investigations with mathematics itself;

◆ understand eight points of the compass; use 'clockwise' and 'anti-clockwise' appropriately, specify location by means of co-ordinates and understand the use of bearings to define direction.

◆ collect, read, process, represent and interpret data.

POSSIBLE ACTIVITIES

Pupils could help to design a data collection sheet on an environmental issue and use it to record a set of data leading to a frequency table. They could construct and interpret bar charts, for example, litter in the playground, green issues, vandalism or graffiti.

Teachers could explore the environmental dimension by providing pupils with opportunities to:

◆ be introduced to the concept of scale in maps and drawings and use the eight points of the compass and the terms 'clockwise' and 'anti-clockwise', eventually using bearings to define directions;

◆ learn to specify location by means of co-ordinates and develop a basic understanding of correlation.

POSSIBLE ACTIVITIES

Pupils might develop mathematical skills of measurement, distance estimation, finding bearings in the environment. Pupils could use data from environmental issues as a source for developing mathematical skills in data handling.

THE POTENTIAL CONTRIBUTION OF SUBJECTS AT KEY STAGES 3 AND 4 TO ENVIRONMENTAL EDUCATION

SCIENCE

KEY STAGE 4

Teachers could explore the environmental dimension by providing pupils with opportunities to:

- make a detailed and quantitative study of a locality, including the investigation of the abundance and distribution of common species and the ways in which they are adapted to their location;

- explore the factors affecting population size, including human populations;

- explore the cycling of the elements and biological materials in specific ecosystems, where management of the ecosystem imposes a duty of care and discuss the compromises which exist in managing ecosystems;

- consider current concerns about human activity, including the exploitation of resources and the disposal of waste products on the Earth and use their scientific knowledge, weigh evidence and form balanced judgements, bearing in mind relevant factors, such as population size, economic factors, industrial requirements, health aspects and the heritage of future generations;

- consider the energy requirements and the social, economic, environmental, and health and safety factors associated with the extraction and manufacture of materials;

- gain an understanding of the essential chemistry associated with desirable reactions, such as manufacturing processes and agricultural practices, and undesirable reactions, such as those associated with corrosion and food deterioration;

- investigate water hardness in order to develop an understanding of its causes and effects and of methods of water softening including boiling, addition of sodium carbonate and ion exchange;

- explore the social, cultural, economic, environmental, and health and safety implications of manufacturing processes, including the effects of changing economic conditions on the suitability of particular processes and the need for pollution control at national and international levels.

POSSIBLE ACTIVITIES

Pupils might investigate the ways energy is generated, beginning with energy generation in Northern Ireland, to gain some understanding that energy resources are limited and to consider the longer-term implications of the distribution and uses of energy resources. Pupils might consider global issues, such as the 'greenhouse effect'.

KEY STAGE 3

Teachers could explore the environmental dimension by providing pupils with opportunities to:

- study a local habitat at first-hand and make use of secondary sources to investigate the range of seasonal and daily variability in physical factors, and the features of organisms which enable them to survive these changes;

- become aware of the need to preserve their local environment and consider arguments for and against planning in their local area, relating environmental factors to human well-being;

- be introduced to the classification of waste products of human activities as biodegradable or non-biodegradable and gain an understanding that the cycling of carbon and nitrogen is made possible by the activity of microbes and other living organisms;

- broaden their study of locally occurring plants and animals and, through this, be introduced to the major taxonomic groups, food chains, food webs, pyramids of numbers and biomass and group organisms on the basis of similarities and differences and to use keys to name organisms;

- consider the effects of pollutants on the health of plants and animals and know ways these effects can be minimised; come to appreciate that industries require raw materials to produce beneficial products and services, and that these aspects need to be balanced against any harmful effects on the physical and living environments;

- investigate the ways in which water resources are managed and, through use of secondary sources and first-hand practical experience, ways of monitoring water purity;

- consider the social, cultural, economic, environmental, and health and safety issues associated with the extraction and uses of materials, and chemical processes.

POSSIBLE ACTIVITIES

Pupils might research the issue of air, land or water pollution, describing the sources and possible consequences of pollution for living organisms and suggest prevention measures, for example, the impact of industrial gas releases, such as sulphur dioxide and carbon dioxide, on the air; the impact of household waste on land; or the impact of fertiliser run-off and silage effluent on rivers and seas.

THE POTENTIAL CONTRIBUTION OF SUBJECTS AT KEY STAGES 3 AND 4 TO ENVIRONMENTAL EDUCATION

TECHNOLOGY AND DESIGN

Teachers could explore the environmental dimension by providing pupils with opportunities to:

♦ become aware of the social, economic and environmental implications of technology and design activities, particularly with regard to the manufacture of products;

♦ recognise that conflict may arise amongst the needs of individuals, society and the environment;

♦ appreciate that a source of energy is required to make products function;

♦ appreciate that the choice of energy sources will depend on factors, such as cost, reliability, performance and environmental effects.

POSSIBLE ACTIVITIES

Pupils could consider the feasibility of recycling household waste and investigate methods for sorting waste into various categories, as part of a project to design a machine for sorting waste products.

Teachers could explore the environmental dimension by providing pupils with opportunities to:

♦ appreciate that the use and manufacture of products can have social, economic and environmental implications;

♦ appreciate that waste materials and by-products of manufacturing processes may need to be disposed of in ways that protect the environment;

♦ appreciate that many manufacturing processes may give rise to conflicts between the needs of individuals, society and the environment;

♦ investigate the physical properties and characteristics of a range of materials and components;

♦ choose appropriate materials and components to manufacture products or systems;

♦ optimise the selection of materials and components against established criteria, such as scale of product, methods of production, and considerations, such as availability, cost, and aesthetic and environmental factors;

♦ gain an appreciation of how the properties of materials may be enhanced by the creation of composites;

♦ appreciate that the choice of energy source will depend on factors, such as cost, reliability, performance and environmental effects.

POSSIBLE ACTIVITIES

Pupils could evaluate the environmental implications of the choice of materials to be used and the nature of the control mechanisms, as part of a project to manufacture a control system.

THE POTENTIAL CONTRIBUTION OF SUBJECTS AT KEY STAGES 3 AND 4 TO ENVIRONMENTAL EDUCATION

HOME ECONOMICS

KEY STAGE 3

Key Stage 3

Teachers could explore the environmental dimension by providing pupils with opportunities to:

- examine the correlation between diet and health and how the choice of food may be affected by a variety of factors, for example, technology and personal lifestyle;

- examine comparative studies on a range of foods to enable an appropriate choice to be made in relation to healthy diets;

- explore choice and care of materials used in the home;

- examine comparative studies on a range of goods to develop the ability to make informed choices;

- examine the effects of consumer decisions on the environment;

- explore the implications of consumer choice on supply and demand;

- understand the effects of living conditions and home environments on family members;

- examine possible viewpoints related to a range of issues;

- examine attitudes and values of self and others in relation to issues.

POSSIBLE ACTIVITIES

Pupils might have opportunities to conduct a survey of householders to investigate the choice and purchase of resources, such as household cleaning materials, recycled paper products, organically grown vegetables.

In carrying out the survey, pupils could take account of the values and attitudes of a random sample of households in relation to the environment and also how these might influence decisions. Similar surveys/investigations could be conducted on issues, such as disposal of waste or use of energy in the home.

Key Stage 4

Teachers could explore the environmental dimension by providing pupils with opportunities to:

- explore how the family can be affected by internal and external factors, for example, environmental, ethical, political;

- examine the role of the family as it relates to future generations, for example, forming attitudes to the care of property, the environment;

- explore the effects of food technology on the diet of individuals and families, for example, pesticides, insecticides, irradiation;

- examine how the choice of food is affected by social, economic, physiological, psychological and environmental factors;

- explore how the availability, choice and management of resources are affected by personal, social, economic and environmental factors;

- investigate the implications of consumer choice on supply and demand and on the environment;

- develop their understanding of the effects of living conditions and home environments on family members;

- examine the validity of the reasons given for adopting particular standpoints in response to issues;

- explore and discuss ways in which responses to issues are influenced by the beliefs, values, attitudes and perceptions of the people and groups involved;

- examine the response of governments and/or national and international organisations to issues relating to the home and family.

POSSIBLE ACTIVITIES

Pupils, as part of a whole-class project, could be given the task of designing an advice booklet for householders on developing practical steps towards an 'environmentally friendly' home. They could explore and offer helpful advice on issues, such as choice of household materials, food, packaging, waste management, energy efficiency and fuel consumption. It would be important for the booklet to include reasoned arguments to support the importance of individuals, families and societies playing their part in caring for the environment.

58

THE POTENTIAL CONTRIBUTION OF SUBJECTS AT KEY STAGES 3 AND 4 TO ENVIRONMENTAL EDUCATION

GEOGRAPHY

Teachers could explore the environmental dimension by providing pupils with opportunities to:

◆ make and record appropriate observations in the field;

◆ acquire knowledge and understanding of patterns and relationships in the physical environment and relate these to the processes involved in the shaping of the natural world;

◆ develop their knowledge and understanding of a variety of environments;

◆ examine the local environment and a variety of contrasting environments from the wider world in order to form an understanding of the variety of habitats that exist and their associated plants, animals, birds and insects;

◆ examine the factors which influence plant growth and the characteristics of an ecosystem, study the links between its elements;

◆ interpret landscapes which illustrate natural, rural and urban processes;

◆ investigate issues relating to the ways in which people interact with, affect and are affected by their physical surroundings involving consideration of conflicting views over the use of resources, including the management of the environment.

POSSIBLE ACTIVITIES

Pupils might survey people's perception of the quality of their environment and compare their findings with data from other places; relate factors, such as acidity, water and organic content to soil fertility in soil samples taken in the field.

Teachers could explore the environmental dimension by providing pupils with opportunities to:

◆ carry out an investigation in the field and make and record appropriate observations from first-hand;

◆ acquire knowledge and understanding of a variety of environments and relate these to the physical and biological processes involved in the shaping of the natural world;

◆ examine settlement patterns and land use in a local context and contrast with other areas of the world in order to understand the physical and human factors which influence the location and growth of settlements;

◆ interpret landscapes which illustrate natural, rural and urban processes;

◆ investigate issues relating to the ways in which people interact with, affect and are affected by their physical surroundings involving consideration of conflicting views over the use of resources, including the management of the environment.

POSSIBLE ACTIVITIES

Pupils might examine how acid rain produced as a result of pollution in one country can damage forests in another country; investigate an issue relating to local pollution, land-use or development in which there is conflict over the use of or the effect upon the environment, for example, the building of a road.

59

THE POTENTIAL CONTRIBUTION OF SUBJECTS AT KEY STAGES 3 AND 4 TO ENVIRONMENTAL EDUCATION

BUSINESS STUDIES

Teachers could explore the environmental dimension by providing pupils with opportunities to:

♦ study the external influences which affect the operation of a business;

♦ study and investigate the regulations and constraints which affect business activity;

♦ investigate the impact of change on the operation of a business;

♦ explore how businesses exist in a local, national and an international context and examine ways in which businesses may be affected by changes in their environment;

♦ develop an understanding of the effects of external influences, including legislation, on production and marketing practices;

♦ identify and formulate a range of aims which a business may have and investigate how these may influence its behaviour;

♦ examine the factors contributing to the growth or decline of businesses.

POSSIBLE ACTIVITIES

Pupils might carry out a survey of the growing sales by large retailers of environmentally friendly products; or research how large manufacturers are using environmental issues as part of their marketing campaigns; or investigate the government legislation which is designed to control, for example, air or water pollution. It might be possible to visit a local firm and investigate the costs to the business of such legislation; contact a number of businesses in their area and ask them for their respective aims in order to find out how many, if any, include promoting a better environment; investigate the growth of businesses which are trading in environmentally friendly products or the decline and closure of firms which had been dealing, for example, in furs.

HISTORY

KEY STAGE 3

Teachers could explore the environmental dimension by providing pupils with opportunities to:

◆ study a School Designed Unit, involving the investigation of an aspect of local history within the context of events and trends taking place on a wider regional, national or international scale, for example

- an aspect of the local community over a long period of time
- an aspect of the local community during a short period of time, or the history of a local site during a specific period
- an aspect of the local community to illustrate local evidence of, for example, Norman settlements or the Ulster plantation.

POSSIBLE ACTIVITIES

Pupils might study the development of a linen mill within the context of the history of the linen industry in Ulster and consider the environmental impact of the linen industry over time, or pupils might study the extant evidence of Norman settlement in the modern environment and consider how and why such environmental features should be preserved, with reference to the successful preservation of the similar environments at a regional, national or international scale.

KEY STAGE 4

Teachers could explore the environmental dimension by providing pupils with opportunities to:

◆ consider the social and economic development of Northern Ireland within the context of the United Kingdom and the causes and consequences of political unrest within Northern Ireland (Core 1);

◆ consider the consequences of the Second World War on Europe and changing relations in Europe (Core 2).

POSSIBLE ACTIVITIES

Pupils might study the environmental effects of war and the policies of environmental restoration. Pupils might compare the effects of industrial development upon environmental pollution in Eastern and Western Block countries and the political, social and environmental issues arising for countries, such as Germany and Russia.

THE POTENTIAL CONTRIBUTION OF SUBJECTS AT KEY STAGES 3 AND 4 TO ENVIRONMENTAL EDUCATION

ART AND DESIGN

Teachers could explore the environmental dimension by providing pupils with opportunities to:

Teachers could explore the environmental dimension by providing pupils with opportunities to:

◆ enrich their sensory experiences and develop aesthetic awareness;

◆ make use of visits to look at the local environment and talk to people;

◆ develop specific skills for recording, using a variety of media and techniques, from first-hand experience of the made and natural environments;

◆ make drawings and take photographs of a variety of different environments.

POSSIBLE ACTIVITIES

Pupils might look at and discuss ways in which advertising signs and hoardings can affect the appearance of the environment before starting work on a poster.

◆ make personal, visual and tactile responses to feelings, ideas and environments;

◆ make use of visits to museums, workshops, galleries, industrial/commercial locations and the outdoor environment;

◆ experiment with various ways of using a wide range of media and techniques with sensitivity and accuracy in their work, and develop specific skills for recording from direct experience of the natural and made environments;

◆ use a wide range of media and techniques, including, where appropriate, overlap, linear and aerial perspective, for recording from direct experience of the natural and made environments.

POSSIBLE ACTIVITIES

Pupils might explore ways in which a derelict building might be transformed into a youth club, identify the needs of young people and describe the image the premises should project; identify design features aspects which might improve the immediate environment; prepare designs, in the form of drawings and overlays, as part of a development plan presentation.

THE POTENTIAL CONTRIBUTION OF SUBJECTS AT KEY STAGES 3 AND 4 TO ENVIRONMENTAL EDUCATION

MUSIC

Teachers could explore the environmental dimension by providing pupils with opportunities to:

◆ become involved in activities which encourage the progressive acquisition of listening, composing and performing skills which will enable them to express, through the music they compose and perform, their ideas and feelings about themselves and the world around them;

◆ perform and listen to music from a diverse range of styles and cultural traditions;

◆ approach music new to them with an open and enquiring mind.

POSSIBLE ACTIVITIES

Pupils might reflect on environmental issues at local and national levels and express their feelings about such issues through the music they compose, in order to understand that music can express feelings which are not always easy to verbalise.

Teachers could explore the environmental dimension by providing pupils with opportunities to:

◆ become involved in activities which encourage the progressive acquisition of listening, composing and performing skills which will enable them to express, through the music they compose and perform, their ideas and feelings about themselves and the world around them;

◆ perform and listen to music from a diverse range of styles and cultural traditions;

◆ approach music new to them with an open and enquiring mind.

POSSIBLE ACTIVITIES

Pupils might reflect on environmental issues at local, national and global levels and express their feelings about such issues through the music they compose, in order to understand that music can express feelings which are not always easy to verbalise.

THE POTENTIAL CONTRIBUTION OF SUBJECTS AT KEY STAGES 3 AND 4 TO ENVIRONMENTAL EDUCATION

PHYSICAL EDUCATION

Teachers could explore the environmental dimension by providing pupils with opportunities to:

◆ develop trust, co-operation and decision-making and an association and enjoyment with being out-of-doors, for example, hill walking, canoeing, camping and rambling.

POSSIBLE ACTIVITIES

Pupils should investigate their impact on the environment, such as the effect of lighting fires, pitching tents, using wood for fires, lighting, leaving litter during outdoor activities.

Teachers could explore the environmental dimension by providing pupils with opportunities to:

◆ pursue activities within a range of environments including forest, hills, lake, river, sea and open country.

POSSIBLE ACTIVITIES

Pupils could investigate the impact of human activities on the environment, for example, the Mourne Walk.

THE POTENTIAL CONTRIBUTION OF SUBJECTS AT KEY STAGES 3 AND 4 TO ENVIRONMENTAL EDUCATION

DRAMA

Teachers could explore the environmental dimension by providing pupils with opportunities to:

◆ come to terms with themselves and the world in which they live and to explore a range of human and cultural issues.

POSSIBLE ACTIVITIES

Pupils might use improvisation to explore the issues involved in the siting of a new waste disposal site from the viewpoints of the developer, local residents, the local council, and an environmental pressure group. Pupils might research a major environmental disaster, such as that at Bhopal and make a dramatic presentation to a class studying pollution. Pupils might use dance drama to illustrate the effect of a storm on a field of corn. They might use mime to illustrate the growth of a flower or the effects of smog on the aged. Pupils might use drama strategies, such as hot seating and conscience alley to explore the opinions and thoughts of someone who has carelessly and/or deliberately poisoned a stretch of river through the release of harmful chemicals.

KEY STAGE

MODERN LANGUAGES

Teachers could explore the environmental dimension by providing pupils with opportunities to:

◆ address the following topics

- the environment, for example, conservation, energy, pollution, noise
- home, town and region, for example, recreation and leisure, local environment, places of interest, directions, industry, local history and geography
- weather and climate, for example, seasons, weather forecasts
- towns and areas of the target language, for example, location, features, amenities, facilities, tourism, industry.

POSSIBLE ACTIVITIES

Pupils might write to a penpal describing attractive features of their own environment or exchange material written in the target language, for example, tourism brochures or literature about an environmental issue.

KEY STAGE

RELIGIOUS EDUCATION

KEY STAGE 3

Teachers could explore the environmental dimension by providing pupils with opportunities to:

◆ investigate and reflect on the wonder of creation, people's record of carelessness in relation to the environment and the challenge to restore the correct balance in nature;

◆ recognise that responsibility for the environment is the concern of the individual and of the local community.

POSSIBLE ACTIVITIES

Pupils might make a collection of newspaper cuttings concerned with pollution and threats to nature and the environment; draw-up a list of ways in which the individual can care for the environment; write a letter to the local council helping it to decide whether local waste ground should be developed either as a factory or as a playground.

KEY STAGE 4

Teachers could explore the environmental dimension by providing pupils with opportunities to:

◆ consider the causes of environmental pollution and possible solutions for the care for God's world;

◆ show evidence of understanding practical Christian responses to problems concerning the environment.

POSSIBLE ACTIVITIES

Pupils might devise a plan to improve the school environment; design a poster to promote awareness of environmental problems, prepare and present a school assembly on the theme of stewardship or prepare a video report on caring for the environment.

SOURCES AND RESOURCES TO SUPPORT ENVIRONMENTAL EDUCATION

6

.... the environmental educator should not
dictate routes for concern
and commitment, but should present
routes to understanding ....
experiences that open doors and
that show glimpses of
pathways that people can follow for
themselves with help and encouragement.

Ordering the Elements:
The Management of Environmental Education
across the Curriculum, D Ebbutt, 1992, World Wide
Fund for Nature UK

THE EDUCATION AND LIBRARY BOARDS

Each of the five Education and Library Boards can support environmental education through their curriculum support services, public and schools library services and the schools educational broadcasts recording services.

Environmental education is promoted mainly through the advisory services of The Environment and Society and Science and Technology Areas of Study. Approaches and provisions differ, for example, through the in-service training (INSET) and resources/facilities available to schools.

Listed below is a range of Field Centres and Outdoor Education Centres offering environmental education support within the Education and Library Board (ELB) areas in Northern Ireland.

Belfast Education and Library Board (BELB)

DRUMALLA FIELD STUDY CENTRE
111 Bay Road, Carnlough, Co Antrim BT44 0HP.
Tel: (0574) 885247.
Comment: This centre offers a wide range of teaching and learning activities in the environment from Key Stage 2 up to A-level studies.
Contact: The Warden

North-Eastern Education and Library Board (NEELB)

BUSHMILLS EDUCATION CENTRE
7 Priestland Road, Bushmills, Co Antrim BT57 8QP.
Tel: (02657) 31599.
Comment: A multi-activity centre where curriculum-based studies and outdoor pursuits are integrated. Activities are cross-curricular, catering mostly for Key Stages 3 and 4.
Contact: The Warden

ENVIRONMENTAL RESOURCE CENTRE
The Causeway School, Giant's Causeway, Bushmills, Co Antrim. Tel: ((02657) 31777
Comment: A joint programme may be arranged involving a visit to the Causeway School and activities along the Causeway coast led by the National Trust Warden at the Giant's Causeway.
Contact: The Warden

South-Eastern Education and Library Board (SEELB)

ARDNABANNON OUTDOOR PURSUITS CENTRE
3 Ardnabannon Road, Castlewellan, Co Down BT31 9EN. Tel: (03967) 78555.
Comment: The programmes are aimed at Key Stage 2 and use a wide range of environmental studies to support the primary curriculum including earth education.
Contact: The Warden

CABRA TOWERS RESIDENTIAL CENTRE
24 Convent Road, Cabra, Newry BT34 5EU.
Tel: (08206) 30315.
Comment: The centre offers earth education activities to Key Stages 1 and 2 using local nature reserves, interpretative centres and forests.
Contact: The Warden

F H EBBITT FIELD STUDY CENTRE
56 Bryansford Village, Newcastle BT33 0PT.
Tel: (03967) 22207.
Comment: Programmes are broadly based to encompass both traditional fieldwork studies and environmental awareness activities.
Contact: The Warden

Southern Education and Library Board (SELB)

KILLOWEN OUTDOOR EDUCATION CENTRE
Killowen Point, Rostrevor, Newry BT34 2AN.
Tel: (06937) 38297.
Comment: Multi-activity centre with environmental awareness permeating its wide range of programmes from outdoor pursuits to A-level studies.
Contact: The Warden

KILBRONEY CONSERVATION CENTRE
15 Kilbroney Road, Rostrevor. Tel: (06937) 38293.
Comment: (Not a board centre but funded by DENI.) Specialises in the earth education programme.
Contact: The Warden

Western Education and Library Board (WELB)

GORTATOLE OUTDOOR EDUCATION CENTRE
Florencecourt, Enniskillen. Tel: (0365) 348888.
Comment: Multi-activity centre with an environmental theme permeating all activities. Earth education programmes also undertaken for schools in conjunction with outdoor pursuits.
Contact: The Warden

MAGILLIGAN FIELD CENTRE
375 Seacoast Road, Limavady. Tel: (0504) 50234.
Comment: Day visit and residential courses available on a wide range of environmental education subject areas. An advisory teacher for primary environmental education is resident to assist with school planning and visits.
Contact: The Warden

Note: Field Centres and Outdoor Education Centres which were established initially by the ELBs to cater for fieldwork and outdoor pursuits now incorporate environmental awareness activities into their courses. They offer pupils quality provision and enriching experiences of different environments through residential and day visit programmes throughout the year.

TEACHERS' CENTRES

Each area board provides resources, materials, support and in-service courses through local teachers' centres. Schools engaging in environmental work have access to this service.

BELB

ULIDIA CENTRE FOR RESOURCES AND TRAINING
Somerset Street, Ormeau Road, Belfast BT7 2GS.
Tel: (0232) 491058.
Comment: This centre houses a video and film library which serves all five area Boards. A catalogue is available which includes environmental material suitable for Key Stages 1-3.

SEELB

SOUTH EASTERN EDUCATION AND LIBRARY BOARD, CURRICULUM AND RESOURCES CENTRE
Grahamsbridge Road, Dundonald, Belfast BT16 0DD.
Tel: (0232) 481111.
Comment: Has produced an action pack called *Team Planet* on our world and ourselves. This pack is designed to deal with the concepts of environment, conservation and development within the context of the geography and science requirements of the Northern Ireland Curriculum at Key Stages 1, 2 and 3. The pack contains four sections (each one can be purchased separately for £4.00, whole pack costs £15.00 plus post and packing) with photocopiable pupil worksheets costing £7.00 per section plus post and packing.

NEELB

AREA RESOURCES CENTRE
28 Railway Street, Antrim BT41 4AE. Tel: (08494) 62254.
Comment: Has produced a number of materials and videos with an environmental content which are disseminated via the teachers centres.

GOVERNMENTAL DEPARTMENTS AND STATUTORY AGENCIES CONTRIBUTING TO ENVIRONMENTAL EDUCATION

There are many governmental departments and statutory agencies which contribute to environmental education. The following agencies have been placed in a number of categories relating to their particular area of environmental education.
The areas are as follows:

♦ general environmental education;

♦ conservation;

♦ pollution and rivers; and

♦ wildlife and forests.

GENERAL ENVIRONMENTAL EDUCATION

Atmospheric Research and Information Centre

Department of Environmental and Geographical Sciences, Manchester Metropolitan University, Chester Street, Manchester M1 5GD. Tel: (061) 247 1590/93.
Comment: Produces a range of materials suitable for use in environmental education. All information free of charge except for videos. A publications list will be sent on request. (s.a.e.)
Contact: Enquiries

Department of Agriculture

ENNISKILLEN COLLEGE OF AGRICULTURAL
Levaghy, Enniskillen BT74 4GF. Tel: (0365) 323101.
Comment: Offers facilities and support for environmental activities especially suitable for Key Stages 1-3. The facilities include a Nature Trail.
Contact: Enquiries

GREENMOUNT COLLEGE OF AGRICULTURE AND HORTICULTURE
22 Greenmount Road, Antrim BT41 4PU. Tel: (08494) 62114.
Comment: Offers facilities and support for environmental activities especially suitable for Key Stages 1-3. The facilities include a Nature Trail.
Contact: Enquiries

LOUGHRY COLLEGE OF AGRICULTURE AND FOOD TECHNOLOGY
Dungannon Road, Cookstown BT80 9AA.
Tel: (06487) 62491.
Comment: Offers facilities and support for environmental activities especially suitable for Key Stages 1-3. The facilities include a Nature Trail.
Contact: Enquiries

Department of Economic Development Northern Ireland (DED)

GEOLOGICAL SURVEY OF NORTHERN IRELAND
20 College Gardens, Belfast, BT9 6BS. Tel: (0232) 666595.
Comment: Information and publications (including maps) on all aspects of Northern Ireland's geology. Suitable for Key Stages 3 and 4. Charges for publications vary; £8.50 per map and £6.50 and upwards for photocopied information.
Contact: Information Officer

Department of the Environment Northern Ireland (DOE)

ENVIRONMENT SERVICE
Calvert House, 23 Castle Place, Belfast BT1 1FY.
Tel: (0232) 230560.
Comment: A range of literature is available free of charge on environmental issues suitable for Key Stages 3 and 4. The Environment Service encompasses the Countryside and Wildlife Branch, the Environmental Protection Division and Historic Monuments and Buildings Branch.
Contact: Information Officer

NORTHERN IRELAND PLANNING SERVICE
Headquarters, Clarence Court, 10-18 Adelaide Street, Belfast BT2 8GB. Tel: (0232) 540000.
Comment: Provides information on divisional branches throughout Northern Ireland. Information available on urban and rural planning strategies. Divisional branches will grant access to sight of local plans free of charge, photocopying extra.
Contact: Information Officer

BELFAST DEVELOPMENT OFFICE
Clarence Court, 10-18 Adelaide Street, Belfast BT2 8GB. Tel: (0232) 540540.
Comment: The Belfast Development Office provides information on Belfast including booklets and a video *The Development of Belfast* appropriate to Key Stages 3 and 4. Some publications will be provided free of charge.
Contact: Information

Department of the Environment (Republic of Ireland)

ENVIRONMENTAL INFORMATION SERVICE
17 St Andrew Street, Dublin 2.
Tel: (010 3531) 679 3144.
Comment: ENFO can provide information leaflets, briefing sheets, fact sheets and action sheets free of charge. The materials include DIY guides on what people can do to improve their environment as well as information on, for example, pollution, acid rain and Radon gas. A reference library is open to the public five days a week. A publications list will be sent on request.
Contact: Information Officer

District Councils (Northern Ireland)

Departments of Environmental Health are involved in aspects of environmental education.
Comment: Literature is available on issues, such as environmental health, waste management and pollution control. Many District Councils promote local initiatives involving schools which generate environmental awareness through project work, for example, litter campaigns, tree planting, displays and production of materials.
Contact: Environmental Health Officer. In Belfast also contact the Education Offices, Parks Department, Malone House, Barnetts Demesne, Belfast BT9 5PB. Tel: (0232) 681246.

European Action for the Environment

c/o CURRICULUM DEVELOPMENT UNIT
Sundrive Road, Dublin 12. Tel: (010 3531) 535487.
Comment: The EAE is an environmental network of twenty-eight schools located in both Northern Ireland and the Republic. The schools work together on environmental projects. As well as that, EAE is also part of the Organisation for Economic Co-operation and Development (OECD) Environment and Schools Initiative which involves schools in nineteen OECD countries.
Contact: Programme Facilitator

Health Education Authority

Hamilton House, Mabledon Place, London WC1H 9TX. Tel: (071) 383 3833.
Comment: Produces an 'Environmental Health' resource list which will be provided free of charge upon request. (s.a.e.)
Contact: Information Department

Lee Valley Park Countryside Centre

Abbey Gardens, Waltham Abbey, Essex EN9 1XQ. Tel: (0992) 713838.
Comment: Produce a wide variety of materials and teaching packs suitable for use with Key Stages 1 and 2. Some of these packs include activities designed for schools, groups and families by the Lee Valley Park Countryside Service. Charges for publications and teachers' packs vary. A publications list will be sent on request.
Contact: Youth and Schools Officer

The Lough Neagh Discovery Centre

Oxford Island National Nature Reserve, Oxford Island, Craigavon BT66 6NJ. Tel: (0762) 322205.
Comment: Indoor and outdoor activities include an exhibition with multi-media audio-visual displays describing Lough Neagh–its formation, settlement, history, and wildlife resources. An 'Ecolab' allows a variety of hands-on experiences. Admission charge.
Contact: Education Officer

Ministry of Agriculture, Fisheries & Food (MAFF)

3-10 Whitehall Place, London SW1A 2HH.
Tel: (0645) 335577 (local rate).
Comment: MAFF produces a wide variety of resources and reading lists. The information can be local, technical or on general issues. The 'Teaching Aids' list gives details of companies and organisations that will supply products/educational information. MAFF also has booklets giving information about farms that could be visited and how to plan such a visit. A publications list will be sent on request.
Contact: Enquiries

MUSEUMS

Local and county museums have collections which include natural history, archaeology and cultural heritage of the local area. The following are some of the larger museums.

ULSTER MUSEUM
Botanic Gardens, Belfast BT9 5AB. Tel: (0232) 381251.
Comment: Produces a leaflet with details of resources for all key stages, including environmental issues, free on request. Provides INSET on various subjects including the environment as well as producing an education pack. Most materials are free of charge.
Contact: Science Education Officer

ULSTER FOLK AND TRANSPORT MUSEUM
Cultra, Holywood, Co Down BT18 0EU.
Tel: (0232) 428428.
Comment: Most useful for cultural heritage studies. Offers residential accommodation. Many environmental activities can be carried out in nearby Crawfordsburn Country Park. Admission charge except for pupils with special educational needs.
Contact: The Education Officer

ULSTER AMERICAN FOLK PARK
Mellon Road, Castletown, Omagh BT78 5QY.
Tel: (03292) 3293.
Comment: Most useful for cultural heritage studies. Resource materials aimed at Key Stages 2 and 3. Admissions charge.
Contact: Education Officer

Northern Ireland Aquarium

The Ropewalk, Castle Street, Portaferry BT22 1NZ.
Tel: (02477) 28062.
Comment: Interpretation and display of marine life of Strangford Lough. A dry display area and a touch tank are available. A teaching pack and pupil worksheets are suitable for Key Stage 2. Admissions charge.
Contact: Education Officer

Northern Ireland Centre for Learning Resources (NICLR)

The Orchard Building, Stranmillis College, Stranmillis Road, Belfast BT9 5DY. Tel: (0232) 664525.
Comment: Produces and publishes a range of materials suitable for environmental education. Titles include *Laganside: A Process of Change* which can be used for geography at Key Stage 3 and includes a video as well as a computer disk. Other titles include *Water: A Precious Resource* and *The Forest Experience: A Teachers' Resource Pack* which is suitable for use with pupils at Key Stage 2 and attempts to develop children's love of nature, the natural world and open spaces. Charges for publications vary; a publications list will be sent on request.
Contact: Information

Northern Ireland Science and Technology Regional Organisation (NISTRO)

University of Ulster, Jordanstown, Newtownabbey, Co Antrim BT37 0OB. Tel: (0232) 365131 Ext: 2682.
Comment: Produces a number of teaching packs and resources suitable for environmental education. These titles include *Energy in The Curriculum–A National Support Service for Schools*, produced and published by NISTRO and supported by The Standing Conference on Schools' Science and Technology; Science and Technology Regional Organisations; The Coal Advisory Service and The Department for Enterprise. Other titles, which include *Design for Living, Airports Technology, Waste Disposal, Waterside Redevelopment, Gardening by Design* and *Water Works with Technology,* are available from The Standing Conference on Schools' Science and Technology, 76 Portland Place, London W1N 4AA. Tel: (071 278) 2468. Charges for publications vary.
Contact: Information

Northern Ireland Tourist Board (NITB)

Headquarters, St. Anne's Court, 59 North Street, Belfast BT1 1NB. Tel: (0232) 231221.
Comment: Provides leaflets and brochures on heritage centres. The NITB recently completed a document, *Tourism in Northern Ireland: A Sustainable Approach,* which looks at the relationship among tourism, the environment and the culture and people of Northern Ireland.
Contact: Publications Section

Ordnance Survey of Northern Ireland (OSNI)

Headquarters, Colby House, Stranmillis Court, Belfast BT9 5BJ. Tel: (0232) 661244.
Comment: OSNI publishes standard mapping of Northern Ireland at scales ranging from 1:500000 to 1:1250, including the 1: 50000 Discoverer Series and street maps covering a number of towns in Northern Ireland. In 1993 a new motoring Atlas of Ireland was published. For further details contact Ordnance

Survey Headquarters or any of the Regional Offices at Coleraine (0265) 43622, Craigavon (0762) 341144 or Omagh (0662) 244659. Charges for publications vary.
Contact: Enquiries

Training and Employment Agency (T & EA)

Headquarters, Clarendon House, 9-21 Adelaide Street, Belfast BT2 8NR. Tel: (0232) 239944.
Comment: Many environmental improvement projects are provided through its Action for Community Employment Schemes (ACE) and Youth Training Programme (YTP) linked to Conservation Volunteers Northern Ireland (CVNI) and Ulster Wildlife Trust (UWT). These training programmes are often involved with school environmental projects.
Contact: Enquiries

CONSERVATION

Department of Agriculture

CONSERVATION AND LAND DIVISION
Dundonald House, Upper Newtownards Road, Belfast BT4 3SB. Tel: (0232) 524567.
Comment: General information on agri-environment policies, for example, on the environmentally sensitive areas in Northern Ireland (Mournes, Glens of Antrim, West Fermanagh and Erne Lakeland), suitable for Key Stages 3 and 4. Most materials free of charge.
Contact: Information

COUNTRYSIDE MANAGEMENT
Room 554, Dundonald House, Upper Newtownards Road, Belfast BT4 3SB. Tel: (0232) 520000.
Comment: Produces a range of material on conservation and other environmental issues. All information free of charge. A publications list will be sent on request.
Contact: Enquiries

Department of Economic Development Northern Ireland (DED)

ENERGY EFFICIENCY SERVICE
Headquarters, Netherleigh, Massey Avenue, Belfast BT4 2JP. Tel: (0232) 529900.
Comment: Guidance material on energy conservation is available for use with all key stages, free of charge,

with particular relevance to Northern Ireland. Other material is adaptable to the Northern Ireland Curriculum.
Contact: Information Officer

Department of the Environment Northern Ireland (DOE)

COUNCIL FOR NATURE CONSERVATION AND THE COUNTRYSIDE (CNCC)
Calvert House, 23 Castle Place, Belfast BT1 1FY. Tel: (0232) 230560.
Comment: Provides advice to the DOE on environment matters. Produces an annual report which is available to schools (fee of £5.00 may be waived). Also produces consultation reports which are available free of charge, such as the Peatland Conservation Strategy. One sub-committee, the Ulster Tree Committee, sponsors 'Tree Week' every year. Materials are suitable for Key Stages 3 and 4.
Contact: CNCC Secretariat

HISTORIC MONUMENTS AND BUILDINGS BRANCH (includes ARCHAEOLOGICAL SURVEY)
5-33 Hill Street, Belfast BT1 2LA. Tel: (0232) 235000
Comment: Wide range of historic monuments and buildings in care throughout Northern Ireland (suitable for all key stages), free entry to public buildings and monuments by arrangement. Monuments and Buildings Record, at above address, provides public access to data/illustrations on man-made heritage.
Contact: Information Officer

Institute of Terrestrial Ecology

Merlewood Research Station, Grange-over-Sands, Cumbria LA11 6JU. Tel: (05395) 32264.
Comment: Produces a wide range of materials relating to all aspects of environmental education, including conservation and pollution. Information free of charge. A publications list will be sent on request.
Contact: Publications Officer

POLLUTION AND RIVERS

Department of Agriculture

WATERCOURSE MANAGEMENT DIVISION
Hydebank, 4 Hospital Road, Belfast BT8 8JP.
Tel: (0232) 647161.
Comment: Deals more with rivers than water. Produces a range of materials which could be used

as part of environmental education including material on pollution and conservation. Information free of charge. (s.a.e.)
Contact: Enquiries

Department of the Environment Northern Ireland (DOE)

ENVIRONMENTAL PROTECTION DIVISION
Calvert House, 23 Castle Place, Belfast BT1 1FY.
Tel: (0232) 230560.
Comment: Provides information on pollution control and community environmental awareness. Will respond to requests from schools and interested groups for speakers on environmental education. Information free of charge. A publications list will be sent on request.
Contact: Information Officer

LAGANSIDE CORPORATION
Clarendon Building, 15 Clarendon Road, Belfast BT1 3BG. Tel: (0232) 328507.
Comment: Provides information which focuses on the Lagan. Resource material, for example, videos and teacher's pack, available for Key Stage 3. Will respond to requests from teachers for materials, speakers and guided tours for school parties free of charge.
Contact: Information Officer

WILDLIFE AND FORESTS

Belfast Zoo

Antrim Road, Belfast BT36 7PN. Tel: (0232) 776277.
Comment: Produces a range of materials suitable for all key stages, particularly on conservation and wildlife. Information packs and videos will sent free of charge. Admission charges.
Contact: Education Officer

Department of Agriculture

FOREST SERVICE
Dundonald House, Upper Newtownards Road, Belfast BT4 3SB. Tel: (0232) 524949.
Belvoir Park Forest, Belfast BT8 4QT.
Tel: (0232) 491540.
Comment: The Forest Service encourages schools to make use of the forest as an 'outdoor classroom'. In addition to organising facilities for schools at Belvoir Park Forest, it has a co-ordinating role between schools and a network of tourist guides based at all major forests across the Province. These guides conduct visiting parties of children and assist teachers in interpreting the forest environment. Information leaflets on trees and identification charts will be sent free of charge.
Contact: Information

Department of the Environment Northern Ireland (DOE)

COUNTRYSIDE AND WILDLIFE BRANCH
Calvert House, 23 Castle Place, Belfast BT1 1FY.
Tel: (0232) 230560.
Comment: Information is available on conservation of wildlife and habitats in Northern Ireland, nature reserves, Areas of Outstanding Natural Beauty (AONB) and Areas of Special Scientific Interest (ASSI). There is a grant scheme for school nature conservation projects. Also available are environmental displays, exhibitions and educational literature at various interpretive centres. The centres, listed below, cover a variety of habitats including river, lake, woodland, bogland and beach. Most provide worksheets, talks and guided tours. Admission is free.

1. Castlearchdale Country Park
   Castlearchdale, Irvinestown, Co Fermanagh BT94 1PP. Tel: (03656) 21588.
   Contact: The Warden

2. Peatlands Park
   33 Derryhubbert Road, Dungannon, Co Tyrone BT71 6NW. Tel: (0762) 851102.
   Contact: The Warden

3. Crawfordsburn Country Park
   Bridge Road South, Helens Bay, Co Down BT19 1LD. Tel: (0247) 853621.
   Contact: The Warden

4. Portrush Countryside Centre
   8 Bath Road, Portrush, Co Antrim BT56 8AF.
   Tel: (0265) 823600.
   Contact: The Warden

5. Mourne Countryside Centre
   91 Central Promenade, Newcastle, Co Down BT33 0HH. Tel: (03967) 24059.
   Contact: The Warden

6. Quoile Centre
   5 Quay Road, Downpatrick, Co Down BT30 7JB. Tel: (0396) 613280.
   Contact: The Warden

6. Ness Wood Country Park
   Contact: The Warden at Roe Valley Country Park.

7. Redburn Country Park
   Contact: The Warden at Scrabo Country Park.

8. Oxford Island
   Craigavon, Co Armagh BT66 6NJ.
   Tel: (0762) 322205.
   Contact: The Warden

9. Roe Valley Country Park
   41 Dogleap Road, Limavady, Co Londonderry BT49 9NN. Tel: (05047) 62074.
   Contact: The Warden

10. Scrabo Country Park
    203a Scrabo Road, Newtownards, Co Down BT23 4SJ. Tel: (0247) 811491.
    Contact: The Warden

ENVIRONMENTAL IMPROVEMENT BRANCH
Clarence Court, 10-18 Adelaide Street, Belfast BT2 8GB. Tel: (0232) 540540.
Comment: Provides, free of charge, information and a database, known as *Nature in the City*, on flora, fauna, and habitats in Belfast. The branch provides a link between local community action groups and schools undertaking practical environmental work.
Contact: Information

English Nature

Northminster House, Northminster Road, Peterborough PE1 1UA. Tel: (0733) 340345.
Comment: Provides a publications and journals catalogue on request. Books include *Wildlife in Towns: A Teacher's Guide* (priced at £2.60) and a slide pack on nature conservation topics (priced at £17.50) suitable for Key Stages 3-4.
Contact: Publications Section

Forestry Commission

Forestry Authority Research Station, Alice Holt Lodge, Wrecclesham, Farnham, Surrey GU10 4LH.
Tel: (0420) 22255.
Comment: The Commission produces a range of materials on environmental education with particular focus on the forest and its flora and fauna. Information will be sent free of charge. A publications list will be sent on request. (s.a.e.)
Contact: Enquiries

NON-GOVERNMENTAL AGENCIES AND VOLUNTARY BODIES CONTRIBUTING TO ENVIRONMENTAL EDUCATION

There are many of these agencies within Northern Ireland contributing at regional and local level with a much greater number operational at United Kingdom and worldwide network level. The following are example of some of those currently servicing schools in Northern Ireland.

The agencies have been placed in a number of categories relating to their particular area of environmental education.

The areas are as follows:

- general environmental education;
- conservation;
- development education;
- pollution and rivers;
- recycling and waste; and
- wildlife and forests.

GENERAL ENVIRONMENTAL EDUCATION

ARK Trust

8 Bourdon Street, London W1X 9HX.
Tel: (071) 409 2638.
Comment: Will supply for a charge of £6.50 an award winning video starring Dawn French as 'Mother Earth'. Also will supply, free of charge, booklets on the things that individuals can do to help protect the environment. These booklets would be appropriate for Key Stages 3 and 4. (s.a.e.)
Contact: Campaigns Assistant

Campaign for Nuclear Disarmament (CND)

162 Holloway Road, London N7 8DQ.
Tel: (071) 700 2393.
Comment: Produce a number of fact sheets on nuclear power, nuclear weapons, the Arms Race and the relationship with, and impact on, the environment. Has a strong youth section which produces materials suitable for use in schools and which is currently updating all education packs. (s.a.e. for information)
Contact: Information Officer or Youth CND

Civic Trust

17 Carlton House Terrace, London SW1Y 5AW.
Tel: (071)-930 0914.
Comment: Encourages protection and improvement of the environment. Co-ordinates an annual 'Environment Week' in May. Produces a range of leaflets and competitions suitable for Key Stages 3 and 4. Some publications free of charge. (s.a.e. for information)
Contact: Environment Team

Common Ground

41 Shelton Street, London WC2 9HJ.
Tel: (071) 379 3109.
Comment: Parish Maps Project is just one of many activities concerning the environment in which Common Ground is involved. It can advise the way in which features of human and natural interest may be recorded on a parish map and displayed. It also can provide ideas for other themes, such as 'Local Distinctiveness'. A publications list will be sent on request. Information on leaflets, which could be used by teachers of all key stages, will be sent free of charge.
Contact: Administrator

Community Development Foundation

60 Highbury Grove, London N5 2AG.
Tel: (071) 226 5375.
Comment: Advises on development of innovatory community and youth work projects, often concerned with environmental improvements. Publishes information and handbooks for various community projects. Produces booklets and leaflets suitable for Key Stages 3 and 4. Some publications free of charge. A publications list will be sent on request.
Contact: Information Officer

Community Service Volunteers (CSV)

237 Pentonville Road, London N1 9NJ.
Tel: (071) 278 6601.
Comment: Produces resources, aimed at young people including those in Key Stages 3 and 4 and

adults, on a variety of issues, for example, local government and participation in decision-making. Produces a number of publications particularly suited to Key Stages 3 and 4 including one giving case studies of environmental work in a school in England. Charges for publications vary. A publications list will be sent on request.

Contact: CSV Education

Conaco/DuPont Services to Education

80 Sherlock Street, Birmingham B5 6LT.
Tel: (021) 666 7018.
Comment: Produces a pack for education called *Understanding Our Environment*. This is a multimedia resource pack, available free on request. At this time the company does not publish any other materials on the environment suitable for use in schools.

Contact: Education Co-ordinator

Duke of Edinburgh Scheme

Northern Bank Building, 109 Royal Avenue,
Belfast BT1 1EW. Tel: (0232) 232253.
Comment: Provides awards based on four areas: expeditions, physical recreation, service, and skills with three levels of achievement: bronze, silver, and gold. This scheme is suitable for pupils at Key Stages 3 and 4 and can, on occasion, make a contribution to environmental education.

Contact: The Director

Educational Project Resources

Education Service, FREEPOST, London SW7 4YY.
Tel: (071) 373 7716.
Comment: This organisation publishes sponsored resource packs which follow the National Curriculum and the key stages. These packs are free to teachers and cover a wide variety of subjects, including the environment. When a pack is produced all head teachers are notified of it and requests can be made to have it forwarded. A publications list is not available since stocks of any particular pack may be exhausted soon after publication.

Contact: Enquiries

English Heritage Education Service

Keysign House, 429 Oxford Street, London W1R 2HD.
Tel: (071) 973 3442.
Comment: Provides teaching resources, including books and videos to encourage the use of the historical environment, suitable for use in all key

stages. Free catalogue will be sent on request. Some publications free of charge.
Contact: Education Service Manager

Environment Council

21 Elizabeth Street, London SW1W 9RP.
Tel: (071) 824 8411.
Comment: Produces a range of materials relating to all aspects of environmental education including pollution and conservation suitable for use in schools. A publications list will be sent on request. Information will be sent free of charge.
Contact: Enquiries

Environment Networks

c/o West Midlands Environment Network (WMEN), 23 Hamstead Road, Birmingham B19 1BX.
Tel: (021) 359 3973.
Comment: Regional Environment Networks can be found in a number of areas. They can be useful sources for local contacts, information and advice on what groups are engaging in environmental work. WMEN can supply details of your nearest Network.
Contact: Information and Training Officer

Field Studies Council

Central Services, Preston Montford, Montford Bridge, Shrewsbury SY4 1HW. Tel: (0743) 850674.
Comment: Runs environmental courses on a wide range of themes for all key stages, A-level and INSET. Also produces publications. School brochures, teachers course leaflets and publications catalogue will be sent on request. Charges for publications vary. (s.a.e. for information)
Contact: Education Adviser

Greenpeace UK

Canonbury Villa, London N1 2PN.
Tel: (071) 354 5100.
Comment: Campaigns about environmental issues throughout the world by lobbying and non-violent direct action protests, which are backed by scientific research. Can provide a publications list which includes a limited number of publications suitable for use with all key stages. Some information will be sent free of charge. Sells products through Traidcraft plc (see below). (s.a.e. for further information)
Contact: Public Information Department

Groundwork Foundation

85-87 Cornwall Street, Birmingham B3 3BY.
Tel: (021) 236 8565.
Comment: The national office for the local Groundwork Trusts which aim to promote environmental improvement through partnership with the public, private and voluntary sectors of society. The national office will be able to give the name of any local trust which may be able to offer projects in which a school could become involved or give advice, identify sources of funding and offer practical support. Contact the national office initially. Some publications will be sent free of charge. (s.a.e.)
Contact: Marketing Manager

Independence Educational Publisher

PO Box 295, Cambridge CB2 2EN. Tel: (0223) 843542.
Comment: Publishes a range of materials related to environmental education which may be suitable for Key Stages 3 and 4. Titles include *Population: A Growing Concern; A Waste of Energy?; Animal Rights; Technology and Change, What on Earth Are We Doing?; Whose Life Is It?* A publications list will be sent on request.
Contact: Enquiries

Institute for European Environmental Policy

158 Buckingham Palace Road, London SW1W 9TR.
Tel: (071) 824 8787.
Comment: Produces a range of materials relating both to the environment itself and legislation which have an effect on the environment. The materials would be suitable for use with Key Stages 3 and 4. Information free of charge.
Contact: Enquiries

Learning Through Landscapes

Third Floor, Southside Offices, The Law Courts, Winchester SO23 9DL. Tel: (0962) 846258.
Comment: Provides a range of services and resources to help schools improve their grounds, for use by pupils, teachers and the community. LTL's interest ranges from play issues to formal study. A free information pack is available which includes a publications list. Charges vary for the publications which are suitable for all key stages. (s.a.e.)
Contact: Information Officer.

Living Earth

The Old Laundry, Ossington Buildings, Moxon Street, London W1M 3JD. Tel: (071) 487 3661.
Comment: This is an environmental charity which focuses on environment and education. Produces a wide variety of material and many teaching packs suitable for use with all key stages. Charges for publications vary. A publications list will be sent on request. (s.a.e.)
Contact: Schools Information Officer

National Association for Environmental Education UK (NAAE)

University of Wolverhampton, Walsall Campus, Gorway, Walsall, West Midlands WS1 3BD.
Tel: (0922) 312000.
Comment: The NAAE is a teachers' organisation promoting environmental education in schools. It produces practical guides, occasional papers, termly journal (three per year) as well as a range of publications suitable for all key stages. A publications list will be sent on request. Charges for publications vary. (s.a.e.)
Contact: General Secretary

National Federation of City Farms

93 Whitby Road, Brislington, Bristol BS4 3QF.
Tel: (0272) 719109.
Comment: Mutual support and information organisation that promotes and gives advice on city farms, community gardens and other projects to provide people living in towns with experience of rural activities. Produces a range of pamphlets, free of charge, which are suitable for all key stages. A publications list will be sent on request. (s.a.e.)
Contact: Administrator

The National Trust

Rowallane House, Saintfield, Ballynahinch, Co. Down BT24 7LH. Tel: (0238) 510721.
Comment: Publications and materials are available on a range of environmental topics suitable for Key Stages 2 and 3. Guided walks are given at National Trust sites along the North Coast. The topics include flora and fauna, their habitats and conservation; seashore life; and natural history of the North Coast and its conservation management (Key Stage 1 through to A-level).
Contact: Education Officer (02657) 31582.

Environmental trails are available at the following properties (Key Stages 2 and 3):

1. The Argory, Dungannon
   Contact: The Education Officer

2. Castle Ward, Strangford
   Contact: The Education Officer

3. Florence Court, Enniskillen
   Contact: The Education Officer

4. Springhill, Moneymore
   Contact: The Education Officer

The Coastal Guardians Scheme (particularly suitable for education for mutual understanding groups), operates at the Strangford Lough Wildlife Centre and the North Coast. It usually involves groups from twinned schools undertaking a range of conservation activities at their allocated stretch of coastline over a twelve month period.
Contact: Regional Education Officer.

Northern Ireland Educational Support Unit (NIESU)

6 College Park, Belfast BT7 1LP. Tel: (0232) 245133 Ext 5123 or 335123.
Comment: Offers support to teachers in post-primary schools. Several panels of teachers produce resource materials, and organise lectures and outings with direct relevance to environmental education. Funding to attend these is available from the Regional Training Unit (RTU).
Contact: Information Officer

Northern Ireland Environment Link

47A Botanic Avenue, Belfast BT7 1JL.
Tel: (0232) 314944.
Comment: Produces a wide range of information on the environment in general and specific topics in particular suitable for use with all key stages. All information on general conservation is free of charge. A publications list will be sent on request. (s.a.e.)
Contact: Enquiries

Open University in Northern Ireland

40 University Road, Belfast BT7 1SU.
Tel: (0232) 245025.
Comment: A wide range of environmental courses and study packs covering local and global issues.

Brochures are available, and many learning materials can be bought over the counter. Charges for publications vary. A publications list will be sent on request.
Contact: Enquiries

Pictorial Charts Educational Trust

27 Kirchen Road, London W13 0UD.
Tel: (081) 567 5343.
Comment: Provides education information free of charge. Produces a range of charts relating to environmental issues, such as pollution and tropical rain forests. Material produced recently is related to the National Curriculum. A catalogue will be sent on request. (s.a.e.)
Contact: Enquiries

Royal Anniversary Trust

PO Box 51, East Horsley, Surrey KT24 6YG.
Tel: (0483) 285268.
Comment: The Trust was set up in 1992 for the fortieth anniversary of the Queen's ascension to the throne. It provides awards for a variety of achievements some of which have environmental associations.
Contact: Enquiries

Scottish Environmental Education Council (SEEC)

Department of Environmental Science, University of Stirling, Stirling FK9 4LA. Tel: (0786) 467867.
Comment: The SEEC is a forum for environmental organisations involved in education and educational bodies interested in environmental issues. It runs a stewardship scheme, costing £10.00 to join, which encourages schools to conduct an environmental audit of their school and provides them with advice on how to go about improving their environment. As part of the stewardship scheme, a teacher's pack is included. (s.a.e. for further information)
Contact: Development Officer

Shell Better Britain Campaign

Red House, Hill Lane, Great Barr, Birmingham B43 6LZ. Tel: (021) 358 0744 or write to FREEPOST, Bangor, Co. Down BT19 1BR.
Comment: Gives practical support to community initiatives in the environment. Provides a comprehensive package of information, advice and small grants. Their *Guide to a Better Britain* is

particularly useful, as it contains both practical tips and a wealth of information about different organisations which may be able to assist in a project. Information will be sent free of charge on request.
Contact: Campaign Administrator

United Nations Association (UNA)

3 Whitehall Court, London SW1A 2EL.
Tel: (071) 930 2931.
Comment: UNA works for global action through the United Nations. It has a youth section and produces comprehensive leaflets on major environmental issues. It produces a number of environmental packs including one which covers the National Curriculum at Key Stages 3 and 4 (cost of £22.00 including photocopiable material) and is currently working on a similar kit for Key Stage 2. Has a number of publications lists including one on environmental issues which will be sent on request. (s.a.e. with an A-4 envelope)
Contact: Sustainable Development Section

Youth Hostels Association (YHA)

Trevelyan House, 8 St Stephen's Hill, St Albans, Hertfordshire AL1 2DY. Tel: (0727) 855215.
Comment: The YHA is well-known for the network of youth hostels all over the country, which aim to provide low cost accommodation. Some specialise in offering activities suitable for groups of young people, such as environmental activity breaks. A *Groups Away* brochure is produced annually giving details of hostels catering for groups (including local attractions, how to get there and activities available). Information will be sent free of charge.
Contact: Customer Services

CONSERVATION

Bord na Mona (Irish Peat Board)

Main Street, Newbridge, Co Kildare.
Tel: (010 353) 45 31201
Comment: Produces some materials suitable for use in environmental education, focusing particularly on peat. Some information is free of charge. A publications list will be sent on request.
Contact: Librarian

Castle Espie Conservation Centre

Ballydrain Road, Comber, Co Down BT23 6EA.
Tel: (0247) 874146.
Comment: Produces a range of materials relating particularly to birds, their habitats and conservation. Some publications are free of charge. A publications list will be sent on request.
Contact: Education Officer

Centre for Alternative Technology (CAT)

Llwyngwern Quarry, Machynlleth, Powys, Mid Wales.
Tel: (0654) 702400/703743.
Comment: CAT tests and demonstrates alternative technologies based on renewable resources at their Centre in Machynlleth. It produces and will supply leaflets which include DIY plans, such as 'haybox cookery' and 'solar water heater' (using a radiator panel) as well as information and resource sheets on renewable energy and organic farming. Charges for publications vary. Some publications are free of charge. (s.a.e. for further information)
Contact: Education Officer

Centre for Research, Education and Training in Energy (CREATE)

Kenley House, 25 Bridgeman Terrace, Wigan 1 5Y.
Tel: (0942) 322271.
Comment: Provides advice and information for all key stages on ways of saving energy. Some information is free of charge. (s.a.e. for information)
Contact: Information Officer

Conservation Volunteers Northern Ireland (CVNI)

The Pavilion, Cherryvale Playing Fields, Ravenhill Road, Belfast BT6 0BZ. Tel: (0232) 644409.
Comment: Publications available on practical conservation work. Will provide advice on creating a wildlife area, grants, plans and labour. Also produces a schools pack (donation of not less than £2.00 required) which is suitable for Key Stages 3 and 4. CVNI also runs an affiliation scheme which cost under £20 per year to join and entitles participating schools to more individual help and advice. A publications list will be sent on request
Contact: Education Officer

Council for Environmental Education (CEE)

University of Reading, London Road, Reading RG1 5AQ. Tel: (0734) 756061.
Comment: Publishes guides to resources for environmental education and a monthly news sheet (cost of £10.00 for ten issues). The Youth Unit promotes and co-ordinates out of school environmental activities, offers advice and produces its own free newsheet called *Earthlines*. A publications list will be sent on request.
Contact: Information Unit

Council for the Protection of Rural England

Warwick House, 25 Buckingham Palace Road, London SW1W 0PP. Tel: (071) 976 6433.
Comment: Produces a range of materials relating to the environment suitable for use in schools. A publications list will be sent on request. Information free of charge if you forward an A4 self-addressed envelope.
Contact: Administrative Assistant

The Forestry Trust for Conservation and Education

The Old Estate Office, Englefield Road, Theale, Reading, Berkshire RG7 5DZ. Tel: (0734) 323523.
Comment: Produces a wide range of materials and teaching packs on the environment suitable for all key stages. The materials are linked to the National Curriculum and specific key stages. Charges for publications vary. A publications list will be sent on request. (s.a.e.)
Contact: Trust Secretary

International Centre for Conservation Education (ICCE)

Greenfield House, Guiting Power, Cheltenham, Gloucestershire GL54 5TZ. Tel: (0451) 850777.
Comment: Provides information on conservation and environmental issues as well as offering publications from a variety of sources. Can provide slide packs, audio-visual material and books. Charges for publications vary. A publications list will be sent on request. (s.a.e. for further information)
Contact: Audio/visual Sales

Irish Peatland Conservation Council

Capel Chambers, 119 Capel Street, Dublin 1.
Tel: (010 3531) 872 2397.
Comment: Provides teaching packs, publications, videos and wallcharts focusing on peat and bogs suitable for Key Stages 2 and 3. Teacher training courses are available on request. Some publications will be sent free of charge, including one produced in conjunction with the Royal Society for the Protection of Birds. A publications list will be sent on request.
Contact: Education Officer.

Royal Society for Nature Conservation (RSNC)

The Green, Witham Park, Waterside South, Lincoln LN5 7JR. Tel: (0522) 544400.
Comment: The national umbrella organisation for the local Nature Conservation & Wildlife Trusts (see Ulster Wildlife Trust below) and WATCH, the junior wing. School group membership (£24.00) entitles the school to take part in national scientific surveys and receive magazines for children and teachers. Local trusts may be able to give advice relating to wildlife and practical management. WATCH initiates various scientific survey projects in an imaginative way that can be undertaken by groups of young people as well as producing an activity pack for WATCH leaders. Charges for publications vary. A publications list will be sent on request. (s.a.e.)
Contact: The WATCH Education Service

Scottish Natural Heritage

Battleby, Redgorton, Perth PH1 3EW.
Tel: (0738) 27921.
Comment: Produces a range of materials relating to the environment, particularly in Scotland, on a number of topics, including conservation. All information on general conservation is free of charge. A publications list will be sent on request. (s.a.e.)
Contact: Information Officer

Soil Association

86 Colston Street, Bristol BS1 5BB. Tel: (0272) 290661.
Comment: Promotes organic food and farming. Can offer advice on how to go about organic farming, also will sent publications catalogue on request. Can supply teaching packs on the environment suitable for Key Stages 1 and 2 for a charge of £5.00 plus £1.00 postage and packing. (s.a.e.)
Contact: Bookshop Manager

The Wildfowl and Wetlands Trust

Slimbridge, Gloucester GL2 7BT. Tel: (0453) 890333.
Comment: Provides educational visits and variety of leaflets, slides and other materials relating to the environment. A teacher's pack is available, suitable for all key stages. A publications list will be sent on request, as will a list of all the Wildfowl and Wetlands Trust centres and details on becoming a member of the Wildfowl & Wetlands Trust.
Contact: Education Department

DEVELOPMENT EDUCATION

Christian Aid

48 Elmwood Avenue, Belfast BT9 6AZ.
Tel: (0232) 381204.
Comment: Produces a few leaflets suitable for Key Stages 3 and 4 raising environmental issues in the Third World. A catalogue will be supplied on request which includes details of audio-visual material.
Contact: Area Co-ordinator

Compassion in World Farming

Charles House, 5A Charles Street, Petersfield, Hampshire GU32 3EH. Tel: (0730) 264208.
Comment: Aims to increase public awareness about the cruelty of factory farming. Produces a range of booklets, leaflets and videos suitable for all key stages. Charges for publications vary. A publications list will be sent on request. (s.a.e.)
Contact: Education Director

Derry Development Education Centre

15 Pump Street, Londonderry, BT48 6JG.
Tel: (0504) 269183
Comment: Provides a wide range of environmental and world development resources and disseminates the materials produced by the aid agencies. A lending library is available along with INSET courses and talks to schools.
Contact: Enquiries

Friends of the Earth (FOE)

26-28 Underwood Street, London N1 7JQ.
Tel: (071) 837 0731.
Comment: Campaigning organisation promoting sustainable development and policies to protect the natural environment. 'School Friends' is a programme launched in 1991 which allows teachers to receive FOE publications free with a once-off payment of £25.00. Provides a wide selection of leaflets giving information on different environmental issues (although some are quite technical). There are a number of packs specifically aimed at schools and a schools catalogue as well as a schools subscription scheme. One pack, *Green Your School,* looks at the school itself from an environmental point of view. Charges vary for the publications. (s.a.e.)
Contact: Education/Information Officer

Henry Doubleday Research Association (HDRA)

National Centre for Organic Gardening, Ryton-on-Dunsmore, Coventry CV8 3LG. Tel: (0203) 303517.
Comment: Researches into organic gardening and horticulture. Useful for technical advice. Undertakes research into reversing desertification in developing countries. Will provide leaflets and other material suitable for all key stages free of charge. A publications list will be sent on request. (s.a.e.)
Contact: Information Officer

Intermediate Technology Development Group

Myson House, Railway Terrace, Rugby CV21 3HT.
Tel: (0788) 560631.
Comment: Provides advice to developing countries in the use of appropriate technology. Has an Education Office which can provide a large number of publications suitable for use with all key stages. Some publications free of charge. (s.a.e. for further information)
Contact: Education Office

One World Centre

4 Lower Crescent, Belfast BT7 1NR.
Tel: (0232) 241879.
Comment: Provides resources for global and Third World studies. A wide range of environmental materials also available for sale or on loan. Most of the major aid and environmental agencies provide materials for the centre. Catalogues will be sent on request.
Contact: Co-ordinator

Oxfam

274 Banbury Road, Oxford OX2 7DZ.
Tel: (0865) 311311. Northern Ireland Branch, 52 Dublin Road, Belfast BT2 7HN. Tel: (0232) 230220.
Comment: Aims to relieve poverty and suffering throughout the world. Produces a wide range of educational materials and posters sold through catalogues, many of which relate to environmental issues. Produces teaching packs for all key stages. Charges for publications vary. Publications and education lists will be sent on request.
Contact: Supporter Services Unit

Survival International

310 Edgware Road, London, W2 1DY.
Tel: (071) 723 5535.
Comment: Human rights organisation that campaigns for the rights of threatened tribal peoples. No junior section, but useful resources. Has special membership for children (at £3.00 per pupil) which entitles them to a monthly newsletter, sticker and badge. Will provide free teaching pack as well as publications list which includes audio-visual materials to hire and purchase.
(s.a.e.)
Contact: Education Officer

Traidcraft plc

Kingsway, Gateshead, Tyneside NE11 0NE.
Tel: (091) 491 0591.
Comment: Sells through a mail order catalogue and directly through voluntary representatives. Products are bought directly from the manufacturers in the developing world and the catalogue has a magazine with information about development issues. Produces a number of teacher's packs, suitable for all key stages. Some kits on how products are made may be borrowed. Charges for publications vary. A publications list will be sent on request.
Contact: Schools Worker

Trócaire

The Catholic Agency for World Development, 50 King Street, Belfast BT1 6AD. Tel: (0232) 238 586 or
169 Booterstown Avenue, Blackrock, Co. Dublin.
Tel: (010 3531) 288 5385.
Comment: Produces a variety of publications on development including environmental issues, suitable for all key stages. The Belfast office has some of the publications in stock, others must come from Dublin. Charges for publications vary. A publications list will be sent on request.
Contact: Education Officer

Water Aid

1 Queen Anne's Gate, London SW1H 9BT.
Tel: (071) 233 4800.
Comment: Aims to help developing countries to establish supplies of safe water and levels of basic sanitation. Produces a variety of resources, most of which are available free or on a loan basis. Produces an education pack for Key Stage 2, *The Dustbin Pack*, and other information suitable for post-primary. A publications list will be sent on request.
Contact: Schools Information Officer

POLLUTION AND RIVERS

Auro Organic Paints

Unit 1, Goldstone Farm, Ashdon, Saffron Walden, Essex CB10 2LZ. Tel: (0799) 584042.
Comment: Suppliers of paints based on plant products, rather than oils. Will supply, free of charge, leaflets outlining the environmental rationale for using paints based on plant products.
Contact: Office Manager

British Waterways Board

Willow Grange, Church Road, Watford WD1 3QA.
Tel: (0923) 226422.
Comment: Manages most inland waterways for recreation and transport purposes. Can provide ideas and information about British waterways. Produces a teacher's resource pack on British waterways, costing £18.00.
Contact: Recreation Manager

Marine Conservation Society

9 Gloucester Road, Ross-on-Wye, Herefordshire HR9 5BU. Tel: (0989) 66017.
Comment: Aims to protect the marine environment and promote its practical management through lobbying, campaigning on issues (including toxic and nuclear waste disposal), research and providing wardens for certain sites. Will provide a catalogue which details a wide variety of leaflets and books, suitable for all key stages, including *The Seashore Code* and *Exploration Seashore* (an activity guide for children) and *The Good Beach Guide*. Local groups may offer opportunities for practical involvement. Charges for publications vary. A free fact sheet pack will be sent out on request. (s.a.e.)
Contact: Enquiries

National Rivers Authority

Rivers House, Waterside Drive, Aztec West, Almondsbury, Bristol BS12 4UD.
Tel: (0454) 624400.
Comment: Produces a range of materials relating to mainly to water, including material on pollution and conservation. Some information is free of charge. A publications list will be sent on request. (s.a.e.)
Contact: Enquiries

National Society for Clean Air (NSCA)

136 North Street, Brighton BN1 1RG.
Tel: (0273) 326313.
Comment: Provides information on all aspects of the environment and produces a wide range of materials ranging from conference reports and surveys to cartoon books for Key Stages 1 and 2. Provides materials suitable for all key stages on a wide variety of topics including the greenhouse effect, air pollution and acid rain. Some information free of charge. (s.a.e.)
Contact: Information Department

Shell Education Service

PO Box 46 Newbury, Berkshire RG13 2YX.
Tel: (0635) 31721.
Comment: Supplies information and teaching aids, mainly on oil-related subjects. Many cover environmental topics. A catalogue of resources and a film and video catalogue will be sent on request. One free copy per school is often provided.
Contact: Enquiries

RECYCLING AND WASTE

Aluminium Can Recycling Association

308, I-Mex House, 52 Blucher Street, Birmingham B1 1QU. Tel: (021) 633 4656.
Comment: Will supply, free of charge, an information pack (including magnetic tester) on how groups wanting to raise money can organise collection schemes. Information pack also includes details of local recycling centres.
Contact: Information Office

British Glass Manufacturer's Confederation (BGMC)

Northumberland Road, Sheffield S10 2UA.
Tel: (0742) 686201.
Comment: The BGMC will give advice on glass recycling and the national bottle bank scheme. It will provide a recycling pack, suitable for all key stages. Information free of charge.
Contact: Marketing Manager

British Waste Paper Association

Alexander House, Station Road, Aldershot, Hampshire GU11 1BQ. Tel: (0252) 344454.
Comment: Produces a limited range of materials relating to the disposal of waste paper. Some information free of charge.
Contact: National Secretary

Industry Council for Packaging and the Environment

Tenterden House, 3 Tenterden Street, London W1R 9AH. Tel: (071) 409 0949.
Comment: Produces a limited range of materials relating particularly to recycling and waste. Some materials suitable for use in schools. Information free of charge.
Contact: Administrative Secretary

NI 2000

Armagh House, Ormeau Avenue, Belfast BT2 8HB.
Tel: (0232) 238532.
Comment: NI2000 outlines the need, and provides funding for, environmental improvement projects in community groups and schools in the Riverside Action Team Area as well as organising on its own behalf all over the province. It gives general advice and assistance to schools concerning environmental matters, particularly on such things as nature areas and recycling schemes. Will provide speakers, if requested, to large groups. Produces information packs for teachers suitable for all key stages. Some information free of charge, others cost £2.00 per pack. (s.a.e.)
Contact: General Manager

Steel Can Recycling Information Bureau

65 Monmouth Street, London WC2H 9DG. Tel: (071) 379 1306.
Comment: Produces a limited range of information relating to recycling and waste. Information free of charge. A publications list will be sent on request.
Contact: Enquiries

Tidy Britain Group

The Pier, Wigan WN3 4EX. Tel: (0942) 824620.
123 Philips House, York Street, Belfast BT15 1AB.
Tel: (0232) 328105.
Comment: Encourages litter abatement and environmental improvement nationally and through their People and Places programme which involves local authorities, schools, industry and voluntary organisations. It produces fact sheets, which will be sent free of charge, on litter, waste and recycling. It also produces other material for all key stages. Charges for publications vary. A publications catalogue will be sent on request for educational material suitable for all key stages.
Contact: Education Officer

Waste Watch

Hobart House, Grosvenor Place, London SW1X 7AE.
Tel: (071) 245 9718 OR (071) 245 9998.
Comment: National project for community-based recycling schemes. Can advise on funding for recycling projects. Produces a free primary pack as well as other packs suitable for Key Stages 3 and 4. Charges for publications vary. Some information will be sent free of charge. Also runs training courses and conferences about the environment. A publications list will be sent on request. (s.a.e.)
Contact: Information Officer

WILDLIFE AND FORESTS

Animal Aid

7 Castle Street, Tonbridge, Kent TN9 1BH.
Tel: (0732) 364546.
Comment: Campaigns to increase public awareness of the abuse of animals in society. Has a youth section and will supply, free of charge, various information and 'ideas for action' leaflets, *Outrage* magazine and an information booklet *Why Animal Rights?* Also available is a video called *Their Future in Your Hands.* (s.a.e.)
Contact: Youth Department

British Trust for Ornithology

The Nunnery, Nunnery Place, Thetford, Norfolk IP24 2PU. Tel: (0842) 750050.
Comments: Produces a range of materials relating to birds, their habitats and conservation. Materials suitable for all key stages. Information will be sent free of charge. A publications list will be sent on request.
Contact: Research Officer

Plantlife

c/o National History Museum, Cromwell Road, London SW7 5BD. Tel: (071) 938 9111.
Comment: Produces a range of materials relating to plants and the environment suitable for use with all key stages. Information on plants free of charge. A publications list will be sent on request.
Contact: Enquiries

Royal Society for the Protection of Birds (RSPB)

Belvoir Park Forest, Belfast BT8 4QT.
Tel: (0232) 491547.
Comment: The RSPB runs a School Group membership scheme of the Young Ornithologists Club (£10.00) which entitles the school to take part in wildlife holidays and day trips. It also produces an extensive range of project guides, most provided free of charge, from Key Stage 1 through Key Stage 4 as well as termly newletters for all key stages. Also provides educational videos to purchase or hire, teacher training and field teaching (KS2 Programme) at Greenmount College of Agriculture & Horticulture. (s.a.e.)
Contact: The Education Adviser.

Ulster Wildlife Trust (UWT)

Ulster Wildlife Centre, 3 New Line, Killyleagh Road, Crossgar, Co Down BT30 9EP. Tel: (0396) 830282.
Comment: The UWT is a member of the Royal Society for Nature Conservation. Schools in Northern Ireland joining the RSNC will be directed to the Ulster Wildlife Trust for local services. It provides school talks and other environmental education services at the wildlife centre. These include a work pack with pupil worksheets and activities and cost between £1.20 and £2.00 per pupil.
Contact: Education Officer

Speedwell Project

Parkanaur Forest Park, 57A Parkanaur Road, Castlecaulfield, Dungannon, Co Tyrone BT70 3AA. Tel: (08687) 67392.
Comment: The Project runs a number of programmes in the forest for Key Stages 1 and 2. These include the forest through the seasons, pond life, wildlife and wildflowers. A fee of £2.00 per pupil per programme is payable. Resource material is provided for use on site. The Project is very popular with schools and there is a long waiting list, so contact should be made well in advance.
Contact: The Director

Tree Council

35 Belgrave Square, London SW1X 8QN.
Tel: (071) 235 8854.
Comment: Gives advice on planting and proper care of trees both in rural and urban settings. Publishes advisory leaflets, suitable for use with post-primary pupils. Charges vary for publication. A publications list will be sent on request. Grants may also be available.
Contact: The Director

World Wide Fund for Nature UK (WWF)

Panda House, Weyside Park, Godalming, Surrey GU7 1XR. Tel: (0483) 426444.
Comment: The WWF promotes knowledge about wildlife and the environment and produces a range of materials suitable for use with both primary and post-primary students. Some publications will be sent free of charge. It operates a comprehensive educational programme for schools, some of which may be of use to youth groups (especially the ideas contained in materials for Key Stages 1 and 2). Some of the publications will be sent free of charge. Charges for publications vary including videos and teaching packs. A full education catalogue will be sent on request.
Contact: Education Department

TELEVISION AND RADIO PROGRAMMES

A wide selection of schools environmental programmes are available through British Broadcasting Company (BBC), Ulster Television (UTV) and Independent Television (ITV) schools broadcasts. Recorded programmes are available through Armagh Teachers' Centre's Audio/visual (AV) Section. The AV Section tapes some non-schools programmes which it believes may be of use to schools. In addition, the Section will tape programmes on request from schools if it is given at least one day's notice. Charges vary for this service.

A selection of programmes available on BBC is listed below. This list is not meant to be complete but does give an indication of what is available.

PROGRAMMES
BBC TV Ulster TV

McGilloway's Way

This series features Olly McGilloway, author and broadcaster, as he travels around Northern Ireland.

THE FOYLE IN SPRING (02.11.92 @ 22.40)
Olly McGilloway traces the course of the River Foyle from Porthall to Mullennan.

HIDDEN TYRONE (09.11.92 @ 22.40)
Olly McGilloway unearths some of the secrets of Tyrone.

CONNEMARA JOURNEY (16.11.92 @ 22.40)
Olly McGilloway travels west to the waters of Corrib.

THE SWILLY HARVEST (23.11.92 @ 22.40)
Olly McGilloway discovers the Fanad peninsula.

THE SHARK HUNT (30.11.92 @ 22.40)
Olly McGilloway sets off from Downings Harbour in search of the blue shark.

MEN OF THE LOUGH (07.12.92 @ 22.40)
Olly McGilloway takes to the waters of Lough Foyle and explores the coastline of Inishowen.

Ulster in Focus

This series increases children's interest, awareness, knowledge and experience of life in their local environment.

THE ULSTER WAY (Wednesdays @ 10.40 Autumn 1991)
Maurice Todd as he travels around the Ulster Way.

THE NATURAL WORLD (Wednesdays @ 10.40 Summer 1992)
A close-up at particular aspects of the natural world.

THE NATURAL WORLD (Wednesdays @ 10.40 Spring 1993)
A look at the sea beneath the waves and between the tides.

RADIO ULSTER

Today and Yesterday in Northern Ireland
This series encompasses features, poetry, music, song, documentary and drama.

ENVIRONMENTAL STUDIES (Wednesdays, @ 11.00 Autumn 1991)
Featuring Cann the Canada goose and birds in Northern Ireland.

OUT AND ABOUT (Wednesdays, @ 11.00 Spring 1992)
Featuring a profile of the Peatlands Park at Birchill.

INVESTIGATING SCIENCE (Wednesdays @ 11.00 Summer 1993)
Featuring the nature of sound, water, and air and wind.

APPENDICES

Erratum

Page 90

The McGilloway's Way series was produced by Ulster Television and not the BBC.

SAMPLE DEFINITIONS OF ENVIRONMENTAL EDUCATION

ROYAL SOCIETY FOR THE PROTECTION OF BIRDS (RSPB)

The basis of their definition includes:

- the means by which people develop awareness and understanding of ecological processes and the Earth's life-support systems upon which all living things are dependent for their survival;

- providing opportunities for pupils to develop and practice skills in problem-solving and decision-making and to make informed rational decisions concerning their own attitudes and behaviour;

- encouraging pupils to make the link between their local environment and its conservation problems and the wider global issues;

- helping pupils to appreciate that environmental problems are inter-related and that one factor affects many others; and

- more than topical 'green issues' and involves understanding the whole environment and should be an integral part of the school's spirit, ethos and management.

From *Environmental Education: The Vital Link,* D M Elcome, 1991. Sandy, Bedfordshire: Royal Society for the Protection of Birds (RSPB)

THE WORLD WIDE FUND FOR NATURE (WWF)

Environmental education enables young people to understand, analyse and evaluate the relationship between people and their surroundings. This is achieved through:

- an understanding of the ecological processes that govern life on earth;

- an understanding of the geomorphic and climatic patterns that influence living things and human activity;

- an understanding of the social and cultural influences that determine human values, perceptions and behaviour; and

- an awareness of an individual's own personal relationship with the environment as a consumer, a producer and a sentient member of society.

From *A Common Purpose: Environmental Education and the School Curriculum,* World Wide Fund for Nature (WWF), 1988 1st edition. Surrey: WWF

The goals of environmental education are:

- to foster clear awareness of, and concern about, economic, social, political and ecological interdependence in urban and rural areas;

- to provide every person with opportunities to acquire the knowledge, values, attitudes, commitment and skills needed to protect and improve the environment; and

- to create new patterns of behaviour of individuals, groups and society as a whole toward the environment.

From *First Steps To Sustainability: The School Curriculum and the Environment,* P Martin, 1990. Surrey: WWF in association with the BBC Education Series, *Where on Earth Are We Going.*

NATIONAL CURRICULUM COUNCIL (NCC)

The objective of environmental education is to increase the public awareness of the problems in this field, as well as possible solutions, and to lay the foundations for a fully informed and active participation of the individual in the protection of the environment and the prudent and rational use of natural resources. (Taken from *The Resolution of the Council and the Ministers of the Council of the European Community*, May 1988. European Community.)

Environmental education aims to:

♦ provide opportunities to acquire the knowledge, values, attitudes, commitment and skills needed to protect and improve the environment;

♦ encourage pupils to examine and interpret the environment from a variety of perspectives – physical, geographical, biological, sociological, economic, political, technological, historical, aesthetic, ethical and spiritual; and

♦ arouse pupils' awareness and curiosity about the environment and encourage active participation in resolving environmental problems.

Taken from *Curriculum Guidance 7: Environmental Education*, NCC, 1990. York: NCC

SCOTTISH CONSULTATIVE COUNCIL ON THE CURRICULUM (SCCC)

Environmental education is an approach which results in actions and activities permeating the curriculum.

This cross-curricular dimension is a basis for learning and teaching not only **about** the environment, **in** and **through** the environment, but also **for** the environment. Environmental education will develop knowledge and understanding of the environment with its many components. The social, cultural and economic aspects of environmental education are interconnected and interdependent.

Taken from *Environmental Education Across the Curriculum*, Curriculum and Assessment 5-14, SCCC, 1993. Scotland: SCCC

CURRICULUM COUNCIL FOR WALES (CCW)

Environmental education has a central role to play in the process of fostering the concerned awareness, active commitment and practical capability that are essential to the future well-being of the Earth and all its inhabitants, both human and non-human. ....

.... Environmental education should help pupils to develop:

♦ **knowledge** of environmental features, systems and processes;

♦ a variety of process **skills**;

♦ **awareness** of various perspectives on the environment and of the ways in which people's circumstances, values and beliefs influence their responses to environmental issues;

♦ positive **attitudes** towards environmental issues.

Taken from *Environmental Education .... a framework for the development of a cross-curricular theme in Wales*, CCW Advisory Paper 17, 1992. Cardiff: CCW

ENVIRONMENTAL AUDIT SCHEDULE

Suggested elements for inclusion in an environmental audit of the school.	To what extent does this reflect the situation in your school? Circle one letter.	What evidence is available to support your responses?
The school has a clearly defined policy statement and code of practice which expresses the schools' commitment to environmental education.	A B C D	
The contribution of individual subjects and cross-curricular themes to the process of environmental education is documented clearly and understood by all involved.	A B C D	
All pupils have first-hand experiences of working both in the local environment and further afield.	A B C D	
Opportunities are provided for all pupils to engage in environmental activities outside normal school hours.	A B C D	
The school encourages participation of pupils in special environmental events and competitions.	A B C D	
The school takes an active and ongoing interest in monitoring local environmental issues.	A B C D	
All aspects of school life support positive environmental messages promoted in the classroom: • care of the school buildings and grounds; • energy efficiency; • recycling; • environmentally-friendly purchasing policy; • disposal of waste.	A B C D A B C D A B C D A B C D A B C D	

KEY   A: Very satisfactory   B: Satisfactory   C: Adequate   D: Less than satisfactory

Statement				
A range of resources is available to support teaching and learning about the environment.	A	B	C	D
Parental support is sought to reinforce positive environmental messages being promoted in the school.	A	B	C	D
There are clearly defined strategies for the co-ordination of teaching and learning about the environment, raising awareness amongst staff and encouraging active participation by pupils in environmental activities.	A	B	C	D
The school grounds are used as a resource for environmental education.	A	B	C	D
There is a planned and structured approach to continuous monitoring and review of the effectiveness of the environmental education provided by the school.	A	B	C	D

KEY   A: Very satisfactory   B: Satisfactory   C: Adequate   D: Less than satisfactory

95

MEMBERSHIP OF THE NICC ADVISORY COMMITTEE FOR ENVIRONMENTAL EDUCATION

Chairperson

Mr O McGilloway   Author and broadcaster

Members

Mr C Barton   Adviser, Environment and Society, Southern Education and Library Board

Mr G F Harte   Chief Environmental Health Officer, Omagh District Council

Miss H Heslip   Divisional Planning Officer, Omagh

Mr S McCarron   Principal, St. Patrick's Primary School, Castlederg

Mr J McCrea   Principal, Ballinamallard Primary School, Enniskillen

Rev Sr A M McQuade   Principal, St Fanchea's Secondary School, Enniskillen

Miss B O'Neill   Assistant Warden, Oxford Island Visitors Centre, Craigavon

Mr A S Orr   Principal, Edwards Primary School, Castlederg

Mr D Scott   Gortatole Residential Centre, Fermanagh

Project Adviser

Dr A Logan   Adviser, Environment and Society, Western Education and Library Board

Project Officer

Mr P Moohan   Head of Geography Department, St John's High School, Dromore

Professional Support

Mr U O'Kane   Senior Professional Offficer (Development) NICC

Appendix 4

ACKNOWLEDGEMENTS

The Environmental Education project was commissioned by the Northern Ireland Curriculum Council (NICC) and hosted by the Western Education and Library Board (WELB).

The Northern Ireland Curriculum Council and the Western Education and Library Board would like to thank the principals and teachers of the following schools for their co-operation and willingness to share ideas and/or materials:

Primary Schools

Bangor Central Primary School, Co Down
Belleek No 2 Controlled Primary School, Co Fermanagh
Castlecaufield Primary School, Dungannon, Co Tyrone
Nazareth House Primary School, Londonderry
St Mary's Primary School, Killyclogher, Co Tyrone
Termoncanice Primary School, Limavady, Co Londonderry
Walker Memorial Primary School, Dungannon, Co Tyrone

Post-primary Schools

Assumption Grammar School, Ballynahinch, Co Down
Clondermott High School, Londonderry
Coleraine Girls Secondary, Co Londonderry
Drumcree High School, Portadown, Co Antrim
Foyle and Londonderry College, Londonderry
Knockbreda High School, Belfast
St Columbanus High School, Bangor, Co Down
St John's High School, Dromore, Co Tyrone
St Mary's College, Portglenone, Co Antrim

Special Schools

Fleming Fulton School, Belfast

The NICC Advisory Committee for Environmental Education would like to thank Mary McCullough, based at Omagh Teachers' Centre, and Jennifer Dorrian, based at NICC, for their secretarial assistance.

Appendix 4

The Council would like to thank the following organisations, bodies and individuals for permission to reproduce extracts from their materials.

The extract from *Greening the Curriculum*, on page 11, is reproduced with the permission of the Committee of Vice-Chancellors and Principals of the Universities of the United Kingdom (published originally by the now amalgamated Committee of Directors of Polytechnics).

The extract from *The Bird of Time: The Science and Politics of Nature Conservation*, on page 15, is reproduced with the permission of Cambridge University Press.

The extract from *Ordering the Elements: The Management of Environmental Education across the Curriculum*, on page 69, is reproduced with the permission of the World Wide Fund for Nature.

The extract from *Environmental Education: The Vital Link*, on page 92, is reproduced with the permission of Mr D M Elcome.

The extract from *A Common Purpose: Environmental Education and the School Curriculum*, on page 92, is reproduced with the permission of the World Wide Fund for Nature.

The extract from *First Steps to Sustainability: The School Curriculum and the Environment*, on page 92, is reproduced with the permission of the World Wide Fund for Nature.

The extract from *Curriculum Guidance 7: Environmental Education*, on page 93, is reproduced with the permission of the Schools Curriculum and Assessment Authority (formerly the National Curriculum Council).

The extract from *Environmental Education .... a framework of the development of a cross-curricular theme in Wales*, CCW Advisory Paper 17, on page 93, is reproduced with the permission of the Curriculum Council for Wales.

The extract from *Environmental Education Across the Curriculum, Curriculum Assessment 5-14*, on page 93, is reproduced with the permission of the Scottish Consultative Council on the Curriculum.

The publishers have made every effort to trace the owners of quotations used in this publication. In cases where they have been unsuccessful, they invite copyright holders to contact them direct.

PHOTOGRAPHS

The Council would like to thank the following organisations and individuals for their kind assistance, and for permission to reproduce photographs:

Pages 10-11, 14-15, 42-42, 68-69, courtesy of **Northern Ireland Tourist Board** (contact Marion McCullough); Pages (iv), 87, 79, 91; Mike Williams (National Trust) , 2-3, 4-5, 37-38-39, 76; Ian Herbert (National Trust) (ii), 83, courtesy of **National Trust** (contact Cathy Lindsay); Special thanks to Doug MacAnally, Education Officer, **Forest Service** (D.A.N.I.).